Singing into Splintered Spaces

Singing into Splintered Spaces

—— *The Rhythms of Mission and Spiritual Discipline* ——

EDITED BY
E. Janet Warren

CASCADE *Books* · Eugene, Oregon

SINGING INTO SPLINTERED SPACES
The Rhythms of Mission and Spiritual Discipline

Copyright © 2022 Wipf and Stock Publishers. All rights reserved. Except for brief quotations in critical publications or reviews, no part of this book may be reproduced in any manner without prior written permission from the publisher. Write: Permissions, Wipf and Stock Publishers, 199 W. 8th Ave., Suite 3, Eugene, OR 97401.

Cascade Books
An Imprint of Wipf and Stock Publishers
199 W. 8th Ave., Suite 3
Eugene, OR 97401

www.wipfandstock.com

PAPERBACK ISBN: 978-1-5326-7880-6
HARDCOVER ISBN: 978-1-5326-7881-3
EBOOK ISBN: 978-1-5326-7882-0

Cataloguing-in-Publication data:

Names: Warren, E. Janet, editor.

Title: Singing into splintered spaces : the rhythms of mission and spiritual discipline / edited by E. Janet Warren.

Description: Eugene, OR : Cascade Books, 2022 | Includes bibliographical references.

Identifiers: ISBN 978-1-5326-7880-6 (paperback) | ISBN 978-1-5326-7881-3 (hardcover) | ISBN 978-1-5326-7882-0 (ebook)

Subjects: LCSH: Christian life. | Spirituality—Christianity. | Missions—Theory. | Missional church movement. | Mission of the church.

Classification: BV4501.3 .S563 2022 (print) | BV4501.3 .S563 (ebook)

11/30/22

Unless otherwise indicated, Scripture quotations are from the New Revised Standard Version, copyright 1989, by the division of Christian Education of the National Council of the Churches of Christ in the United States of America. Used by permission. All rights reserved worldwide.

The Scripture marked RSV it taken from the Revised Standard Version of the Bible, copyright © 1946, 1952, and 1971 National Council of the Churches of Christ in the United States of America. Used by permission. All rights reserved worldwide.

The Scripture marked MSG is taken from The Message, copyright © 1993, 1994, 1995, 1996, 2000, 2001, 2002. Used by permission of NavPress Publishing Group.

Contents

List of Contributors | vii

Preface and Acknowledgments | ix

Introduction | xi
—E. Janet Warren

1 The Discipline of Cruciformity: Civil Religion and the Missional Power of the Cross | 1
—Michael J. Gorman

2 For the Good of the City: The Practice of Missional Discipleship | 17
—Dave Witt

3 Joining Jesus: Prayer as Mission and the Mission of Prayer | 31
—Michael P. Knowles

4 Being Equipped for Every Good Work: Scripture Study and the *Missio Dei* | 44
—Seán McGuire

5 Taste and See: Mindfulness as a Means to a Missional Heart | 59
—E. Janet Warren

CONTENTS

6 Fire and Stars: Neighborhood Engagement as a Spiritual Discipline | 73
—Aaron Smith

7 Loitering with Intent: Hospitality, Prayer, and Encountering the Other | 86
—Jill Weber

8 Chimes of Redemption: Prayer Walking and the House of the Lord | 96
—Peter Tigchelaar

Conclusion | 105
—E. Janet Warren

Contributors

Michael J. Gorman holds the Raymond E. Brown Chair in Biblical Studies and Theology at St. Mary's Seminary & University in Baltimore, Maryland. He is the author of nearly twenty books, including *Cruciformity: Paul's Narrative Spirituality of the Cross* and *Reading Revelation Responsibly*.

Michael P. Knowles, a graduate of Wycliffe College and the Toronto School of Theology, holds the Hurlburt Chair of Preaching at McMaster Divinity College in Hamilton, Ontario. In addition to articles in Old Testament, New Testament, intertestamental studies, pastoral theology, homiletics, and evangelism, his publications include two edited volumes and five studies on the theology of preaching. Most recently, *Of Seeds and the People of God: Preaching as Parable, Crucifixion, and Testimony* (2015) and *Third Voice: Preaching Resurrection* (2021) address the spirituality of preaching in light of Jesus's crucifixion and resurrection. Dr. Knowles is ordained within the Anglican Church of Canada.

Seán McGuire is the pastor of Wentworth Baptist Church in downtown Hamilton, Ontario, and is a candidate in the doctor of practical theology program at McMaster Divinity College. His work focuses on the practice of biblical interpretation, with an aim to equip readers to better think through how they interpret the biblical text. Seán lives in Hamilton with his wife, Jessica, and their children.

CONTRIBUTORS

Aaron Smith has lived and ministered among the urban poor in Manila, Philippines, since the late 1990s. He currently serves as the assistant pastor of the church he helped plant, and at Asian Theological Seminary as the program director for transformational urban leadership. He has published several books including *Visions of Urban Transformation* and *Slums Reimagined*.

Peter Tigchelaar is a husband, father, songwriter, and Benedictine oblate who freely brings his living stone gifting to his hometown, Hamilton, Ontario. He has made five recordings including *World Without End* (a first volume of Psalm settings) and four albums of his original songs—*Wings Meeting Wind* (1994), *Gracious Window* (2009), *More Like Lightning* (2012), and *Better Things* (2014).

E. Janet Warren is an independent scholar in theology and a family physician who practices psychotherapy. Her research interests include the integration of science, especially psychology, and theology. Janet lives and works in Hamilton, Ontario. Her publications include *Cleansing the Cosmos: A Biblical Model for Conceptualizing and Counteracting Evil* and *All Things Wise and Wonderful: A Christian Understanding of How and Why Things Happen in Light of COVID-19*.

Jillian Weber serves on the international leadership team of 24/7 Prayer and is global convener of the Order of the Mustard Seed, a lay, ecumenical religious order. She also serves Emmaus Road Church as their director of spiritual formation. Jill is a spiritual director, regular contributor to the Lectio 365 Daily Devotional app, and author of *Even the Sparrow: A Pilgrim's Guide to Prayer, Trust, and Following the Leader*.

Dave Witt works as a missional network developer for International Teams Canada. For the past seventeen years he has partnered with a group of churches in Hamilton, Ontario to develop the TrueCity network. Dave met his wife Alison while serving for ten years as a missionary in the Philippines. They enjoy calling the ever-evolving diversity of Hamilton's North End home. Dave is currently pursuing his doctorate in practical theology at McMaster Divinity College.

Preface and Acknowledgments

This book owes its beginnings to Matthew Lowe, who developed its vision and recruited some of the authors. For various reasons he was unable to complete the project and passed it on to me. I would like to thank Matt for his inspiration and groundwork.

The book is written in an accessible style with academic details available in the footnotes. Thanks to all the contributors for their cooperation and patience—I have learned much about the process. Michael Knowles was especially helpful in providing feedback on my chapters, and Seán McGuire assisted with proofreading. I also greatly appreciate the unexpected editorial advice given by John Bowen—unrelated to his endorsement! And, of course, thanks to the team at Wipf and Stock.

Finally, note that royalties from sales of this book will be donated to TrueCity and other ministries mentioned in this volume.

Introduction

E. JANET WARREN

COMMENT OVERHEARD DURING AFTER-CHURCH fellowship: "I don't understand those Christians who are so busy doing good that they don't even have time to stop and pray, to be still and listen to the voice of Jesus. How can they replenish their spiritual energy if they don't rest? How can they be co-workers with God if they don't spend time with him?"

And another: "I don't understand people who spend so much time in prayer or go away on silent retreats for a week. Sure, prayer is good, but we should be acting! Doing the work of Jesus in feeding the hungry, going on missions, helping the homeless, spreading the good news . . . "

Well, the other good news is that both are correct. Jesus exemplified and taught both spiritual discipline and mission. Christian discipleship involves both worship and work, prayer and practice, solitude and socialization, imagination and intention. The church sometimes falsely dichotomizes inward and outward expressions of faith. The first may bring to mind monasticism, spiritual disciplines, prayer, contemplation; the second is associated with evangelism, caring ministries, social justice, mission, creation care. Both camps may be tempted to judge the other—too much time in silence and solitude, withdrawal from the world; excessive immersion in the world, not enough time in prayer.

This problem is compounded by the fast-paced, self-centered, and technology-focused nature of our contemporary Western world—a world that craves meaning but remains fragile and fractured. It is also compounded by ambiguities and misunderstandings about the natures of and needs for mission, spirituality, and spiritual disciplines. I will expand on these shortly, but first some more good news. In the past few decades there has been renewed interest in spiritual disciplines and intentional spiritual practices, evident in the new monastic movement, for example. There has also been a shift in the practice and study of mission to incorporate spirituality. Indeed, many local ministries include both of these.

One such example is called TrueCity: a network of approximately eighteen congregations in Hamilton, Ontario, that come "together for the good of the city."[1] TrueCity is congregationally based and neighborhood engaged. Those involved aim for authenticity and active, cooperative involvement with both local communities and the city of Hamilton. They believe, "We grow in Christ as together we engage in his work. Jesus meets us and takes us deeper in our walk with him as we get involved in the work that He is doing." Activities include hosting worship-and-service events for the city's youth and university students, cooperatively assembling and distributing school supplies for low-income families each fall and hampers of food during each Advent season, prayer walks, and an annual conference. I have particularly appreciated the conferences, where denominational differences are set aside as we worship, learn, and grow together. There is a healthy balance between promotion of local mission and ministry needs and time spent in prayer and contemplation. A specific space is set aside for prayer, including forty-eight-hour vigils. An exhibition hall showcases ministries, such as A Rocha (a creation care organization), the 541 Eatery and Exchange (a nonprofit café that operates on a pay-it-forward principle), Helping Hands Street Mission, Christians Against Poverty, Foster Care Ambassadors, and even local educational institutes.

In later chapters we will hear stories about TrueCity and affiliated organizations along with theological reflection on the interface between spiritual discipline and mission. In addition to contributing to the growing literature on the subject, our aim is to challenge fellow believers to better understand and practice rhythms of spirituality and mission, to live counterculturally, and to sing to a splintered world that desperately needs a new song. In this introductory chapter, I will review some current conceptions of mission and spirituality before providing an outline of the book. Let's first look at what the author of our faith says on the subject.

---

1. TrueCity, "TrueCity."

The Rhythms and Teachings of Jesus

"After he had dismissed the crowds, he went up the mountain by himself to pray" (Matt 14:23). In his ministry, Jesus models both inward and outward practices. Prayer often precedes action. Solitude precedes kingdom expansions.[2] The best-known examples occur at the beginning and the end of his ministry. After his baptism, Jesus is sent to the desert alone, resisting the devil by relying on Scripture and the Spirit (Mark 1:11–13). Immediately afterward he proclaims the gospel, teaches his disciples, expels a demon, and heals a sick woman (Mark 1:14–34). The anguished prayer in the garden of Gethsemane (Mark 14:32–42) precedes the prolonged crucifixion of Christ (Mark 14:53—16:8), which, of course, accomplishes salvation for all who believe (Mark 16:8). Another key event is the transfiguration: Jesus and a select few of his followers ascend to a mountain away from crowds where they listen in silence (Mark 9:2–13). God reveals his glory and affirms Jesus as his son. Following this event, Jesus descends, heals a demonized boy, and educates his disciples about spiritual practices and their mission (Mark 9:14–50).

There are many other times when Jesus practices spiritual disciplines and then engages in missionary activity. He spends time alone in prayer and meditation (e.g., Mark 1:35) and quiet time with the disciples (Mark 6:30–33); he fasts (Matt 4:2) and prays for guidance (Mark 14:36). The Father and the Holy Spirit authorize, affirm, and comfort him. This enables Jesus to advance the kingdom, welcome and forgive sinners, heal the sick, expel evil spirits, feed multitudes, and perform many other deeds. Throughout the Gospels we see a rhythm—a back-and-forth of Jesus engaging in spiritual practices, such as silence and solitude, then engaging in ministry and mission, proclamation and compassion. He allocates both space (e.g., garden, mountain, river, desert) and time (e.g., forty days, early morning, all night) for spiritual practices.

Jesus also educates his disciples about the intertwining of spirituality and mission.[3] In his famous sermon on the mount, he explains how to pray (Matt 6:5–13; 7:7–11) and fast (Matt 6:16–18). These are related to teachings about loving and forgiving our enemies (Matt 6:14, 15; 7:1–5), and giving alms in secret (Matt 6:2–4). Jesus uses metaphors such as

---

2. Notable in Mark's Gospel. Jensen has helpful tables summarizing Jesus's rhythms of spirituality and mission; *Subversive Spirituality*, 83–93.

3. Jensen, *Subversive Spirituality*, 95–110.

salt and light, or fruit from a tree, to help his disciples understand that spreading the gospel starts from within (Matt 5:13–15; 7:15–20). Who we are inside is reflected on the outside. Perhaps the classic passage on the connection between spiritual discipline and mission is John 15:1–11. Jesus, the true vine, commands us to abide in him so that we may bear fruit. The spiritual practices of prayer, studying God's word, and dwelling in his love are necessary for us to bear faithful witness, and to participate in God's work and Jesus's life.[4]

New Testament teaching follows the principles of the Old Testament regarding rhythms of spirituality and mission (e.g., rituals, festivals), but redefines some and develops new ones. Jesus attends synagogue on the Sabbath but heals a man's hand, contradicting Jewish law (Matt 12:9–14). He later teaches his disciples the spiritual practice of breaking bread and drinking wine as a sign of the new covenant (Luke 22:14–23). The early followers of Christ also interconnected spiritual practices and mission. They gathered for prayer, praise, teaching, breaking bread, and sharing their possessions (Acts 2:42–47). At one point they divided tasks among themselves; some helping widows in need, others spending time in prayer (Acts 6:1–6). Paul, who exemplified mission, continues the teaching of Jesus regarding spiritual practices; he emphasizes the need to honor the Lord's supper (1 Cor 11:20–34) and to pray without ceasing (1 Thess 5:17). James (5:13–18) teaches that prayer itself can lead to healing.

Rhythms and intertwining are also evident in the complex relationship between divine initiative and human responsibility. In his teaching about the vine and its branches, Jesus teaches about mutuality and mission: "Those who abide in me and I in them bear much fruit" (John 15:5; see also John 6:56; 14:20; 17:20–24). There is mysterious harmony between us abiding in Christ and him in us. Paul also describes this tension: "Now that you have come to know God, or rather to be known by God" (Gal 4:9). We are saved only through God's gracious gift, but we need to accept this gift through faith (Eph 2:8). God initiates the call; we respond in obedience. We work out our salvation daily (Phil 2:12) both by engaging in spiritual practices and by following Christ's command to spread the good news (Matt 28:19–20).

The model and teachings of Jesus on the intertwining of spirituality and mission has been followed to varying degrees and in various ways throughout the history of Christianity. But it is often challenging to know

---

4. E.g., Jensen, *Subversive Spirituality*, 103.

how to apply these teachings in our own contexts. Scripture needs to be freshly interpreted and practiced, without compromise, to meet the needs of our current situations. And our world is needy indeed.

Splintered Spaces and Other Problems in Contemporary Western Society

It is unlikely that anyone is unaware of the high-tech, high-speed nature of our society. Physical and psychological side effects of excessive screen time are well known,[5] and the condition "hurry sickness" is now used to describe those who continually feel rushed and behind schedule.[6] Life has been reduced to "things to do" and "stuff to use." This naturally results in disorientation and feelings of emptiness that need to be filled with more things to do . . . .[7]

Christians are not immune. Many contemporary worship services are filled with busyness and high-tech sights and sounds. This comes with a cost. Interestingly, one cited reason why young people are leaving churches is that they think worship services and teaching are shallow and not always relevant.[8] Of course, technology is not all bad. As we experienced during the 2020 pandemic, it has enabled us to connect with each other to some degree despite social isolation. Nevertheless, we need to use technology wisely.[9] We also need to be cognizant of when and how our Christian beliefs and behavior should be countercultural. There is a spiritual splintering within and without that yearns for a new song.

Many scholars argue that these problems developed following the industrial revolution and the Enlightenment period, both of which are associated with modernism. Postmodernism has accentuated many of these

---

5. E.g., insomnia, obesity, anxiety, developmental delays; effects are more common in children. Strasburger et al., "Health Effects."

6. The term was coined by cardiologists, Friedman and Rosenman (*Type A Behavior and Your Heart*) in 1974.

7. This emptiness is also a factor in substance and behavioral addictions; e.g., May, *Addiction and Grace*, esp. 1–20.

8. According to extensive research conducted by David Kinnaman; e.g., Kinnaman and Hawkins, *You Lost Me*. Jensen suggests that spiritual hunger is strongest within the millennial generation; *Subversive Spirituality*, 213–57.

9. For discussion and guidance on this, see Crouch, *Tech-Wise Family*; Gay, *Modern Technology*.

issues.[10] The above problems are concerning, particularly from a Christian perspective. First, the wonder of technology can lead to idolatry. We worship gadgets and information instead of the true God. Second, with machines to do mundane work, humans have more free time. This has both positive and negative consequences. We may find ourselves without purpose in life. Interestingly, the term "boredom" only appeared in English dictionaries in 1845; related to the term "bored," or "suffering from ennui."[11] Third, the emphasis on reason, empiricism, individuality, and humanism—characteristic of Enlightenment philosophy—fosters a loss of the imagination, narrative, and the spiritual dimension of life, as well as a neglect of care and concern for others.[12] Banality and self-centeredness, quite the opposite of the rich gospel message, make one prone to a shallow, dull existence. We have also lost our sense of mystery and awe in favor of literalistic interpretations of what we read. Fourth, the materialism, consumerism, tolerance, relativism, and pluralism that are associated with postmodernism has furthered this spiritual void. People end up trapped within a cycle of yearning for truth but instead filling themselves with false beliefs and actions.[13] Finally, technology has advanced well beyond that imagined during the Industrial Revolution. Overstimulation from constant interaction with it can make the real world seem dull and lifeless.[14] As the "teacher" comments with reference to those who live apart from God, "Everything is meaningless. What do people gain from all their labors at which they toil under the sun?" (Eccl 1:2a–3).

Theologian Jonathan Wilson, following Alasdair McIntyre, argues that our world is fragmented—akin to a postapocalyptic world in which we only have access to half a book.[15] This is especially true with respect to

---

10. Of course, these concepts are complex, variously defined, and much debated. Briefly, in sociology and philosophy, modernity began in the nineteenth century, and its assumptions of certainty, progress, and autonomy started to be questioned in the mid- to late-twentieth century. E.g., Bosch, *Believing in the Future*, 5–25; Middleton and Walsh, *Truth Is Stranger*, esp. 7–79.

11. Online Etymology Dictionary, s.v. "bored," https://www.etymonline.com/search?q=bored.

12. E.g., Pearcey, *Total Truth*; Middleton and Walsh, *Truth Is Stranger*; Coakley, "Introduction"; McGilchrist, *Master and His Emissary*.

13. E.g., Middleton and Walsh, *Truth Is Stranger*; Block et al., *An Other Kingdom*.

14. Gay, *Modern Technology*, 181, discussing Crouch, *Tech-Wise Family*, 139–53.

15. Wilson, *Living Faithfully*, esp. 13–27. He argues that the church needs to be the rock amidst our morally fragmented society and suggests that new monastic practices may help us to live faithfully within this fragmentation; 50–56.

morality. Without a cohesive community, history, and tradition, we lack a unifying narrative to guide our lives, and wander aimlessly. Somewhat similarly, Paul Jensen suggests that contemporary society has experienced a space-time collapse.[16] Prior to the invention of the mechanical clock and the commercialization of time, used in factory work and train schedules, for example, there were natural seasons and rhythms to life, and spaces that were designated for specific purposes, especially communal gatherings. Now, with the timeless internet and mobile devices that can be with us 24/7, we live our lives anywhere, anytime. Space and time become amalgamated, leading to conditions like "hurry sickness," addictions, and loneliness.[17] We are dislocated and directionless. We hunger for meaning and structure. Interestingly, in 1978, prior to the development of the internet and cellular technology, Richard Foster noted that "superficiality is the curse of our age."[18]

Wilson and Jensen use the terms "fragmentation" and "collapse"—I suggest that the term "splintered" is also a suitable description of our internal and external spaces. This metaphor connotes fracturing and fragility but also implies pain. When we experience splinters, we hurt and seek healing. Predictably, Wilson and Jensen encourage community and spiritual practices as ways to counteract these problems and to repair the splintered spaces that result from living busy yet empty lives.

Singing and Other Aspects of Spirituality

"Swing low, sweet chariot; Coming for to carry me home. . . ." This classic African American hymn, based on the story of Elijah's ascent to heaven, had an eschatological dimension essential for the faith of slaves, but it also probably had a metaphorical meaning—the chariot referring to the underground railroad.[19] Christian spirituality and singing intertwined.

Music is a ubiquitous part of Christian spirituality. From Miriam's celebration of the Exodus, Mary's song of praise, and Paul's encouragement

---

16. Jensen, *Subversive Spirituality*, 31–69; he suggests this collapse began in the 1950s.

17. Jensen notes that these problems have also been recognized in secular society; *Subversive Spirituality*, 40–60. He references Putman, *Bowling Alone*, and Lasch, *Culture of Narcissism*. I would add that decentralization was accentuated during the 2020 pandemic.

18. Foster, *Celebration of Discipline*, 1; the original version was published in 1978.

19. Smith, "Spiritual Wisdom."

to sing spiritual songs, to the rich hymnody of the community of Christ that we have today, singing has both inward (communion with God) and outward (corporate worship and evangelism) dimensions. It also has metaphorical dimensions. Singing can represent both the ways that we practice our spirituality and the ways that we practice mission. Thus, we can sing into a splintered world.

Spirituality, although ingrained in Scripture, is surprisingly difficult to define. It is the entirety of our lived relationship with the Lord, the outworking of our faith, the search for authentic Christian living. It is personal and communal, rational and experiential, a feast and a struggle.[20] Christian spirituality is Trinitarian, creational, incarnational, cruciform, liturgical, ethical, vocational, and revelational. It is "God's passionate embrace of us; our passionate embrace of God."[21] It is the way "Spirit" speaks to "spirit."

Spirituality relates to spiritual formation, transformation, and discipleship.[22] These terms describe the process of becoming more fully united to Christ. We are promised a new heart and spirit (Ezek 36:26), given living water that leads to eternal life (John 4:14), and clothed with Christ (Gal 3:27; Col 3:10). As we "contemplate the Lord's glory," we are "transformed into his image with ever-increasing glory" (2 Cor 3:18). Spiritual formation refers to the processes through which, guided by the Holy Spirit (Rom 8:14; Gal 5:18), our hearts, minds, spirits, and character are shaped and renewed. This process involves all aspects of our selves but it is not just personal; it is not a self-improvement project. Rather, spiritual transformation leads to mission and the expansion of God's kingdom.

The process of spiritual transformation is not easy. We work out our salvation "with fear and trembling" (Phil 2:12). Partly for this reason, spiritual practices or disciplines, based on biblical teaching and the model of Jesus, have become central to Christian life. They are practical guides to aid in spiritual formation. They help us to present our "bodies as a living sacrifice" and be "transformed by the renewing" of our minds (Rom 12:1, 2); to set our minds on Spirit, not the flesh (Rom 8:1–17; Gal 5:16–26). Discipline in common usage implies hard work, self-control, or punishment. But the term originates with the Latin word *discipulus*, meaning pupil. Followers of

---

20. Howard, *Brazos Introduction*, 13–37; McGrath, *Christian Spirituality*, 2–5, 88–108.

21. Webber, *Divine Embrace*, 16, 44–45.

22. E.g., Howard, *Brazos Introduction*, 229–98.

Christ—disciples—are to humbly submit to his teaching, to surrender their will to his. This may or may not require discipline in the usual sense.[23]

Spiritual practices have been written about through the ages and have received renewed attention in the past few decades, perhaps as a result of the increasing disillusionment with shallow Christianity.[24] They are variously understood and classified, but perhaps the best known is that of the popular Quaker author, Richard Foster.[25] He discusses "classical" spiritual disciplines, named not just because of their history but because of their importance. They are a "path of disciplined grace"; both a gift and requiring something of us (recall the tension between divine initiative and human responsibility). Foster cautions against turning them into laws as the Pharisees did.[26] Paradoxically, disciplines lead to freedom. Foster categorizes them in three groups:

- **Inward Disciplines:**
    - Meditation—involving listening to and obeying God, developing a friendship with Jesus; a process of attachment, not detachment
    - Prayer—a central discipline leading us into communion with God
    - Fasting—a practice of abstaining from something, usually food; it is tied to prayer and advisable to start slowly
    - Study—reading and learning about God's Word

---

23. Willard notes that, in contrast to hard work, our "yoke can be easy when we live as Jesus lived in all aspects of his life"; *Spirit of the Disciplines*, 10. However, because some teaching on spiritual formation implies rigid structure, "rules," and "discipline," Ruth Haley Barton uses the phrase "spiritual rhythms" instead; *Sacred Rhythms*, 14–15.

24. Willard, *Spirit of the Disciplines*, 19–24. A recent series on ancient practices includes titles on prayer, fasting, tithing, the sacred meal, and the Sabbath; e.g., McLaren, *Finding Our Way*. Critics are concerned about the popularity of spiritual practices, claiming that they go beyond biblical teaching; e.g., Carson, "Spiritual Disciplines." I suggest that any tendency toward idolatry can be mitigated through prayer for wisdom, and by seeking guidance from Christian communities.

25. Foster, *Celebration of Discipline*, see also, *Freedom of Simplicity*.

26. Foster, *Celebration of Discipline*, 2–10.

- **Outward Disciplines:**
  - Simplicity—a lived expression of an inner desire to seek God's kingdom above possessions and other distractions
  - Solitude—a state of mind and heart associated with silence and listening
  - Submission—the practice of taking up our cross and giving up the need to get our own way
  - Service—the act of quietly, humbly caring for the needs of others

- **Corporate Disciplines:**
  - Confession—the practice of acknowledging our sin to others, involving an examination of our conscience
  - Worship—the essential, experiential response to the only God who is worthy
  - Guidance—the communal practice of seeking the leading of the Spirit
  - Celebration—the joyful expression of Christian life, involving singing, dancing, laughing, and shouting

Evangelical Dallas Willard, also a popular author, divides spiritual disciplines into those of abstinence and those of engagement. The first category can help us to "abstain from the desires of the flesh that wage war against the soul" (1 Pet 2:11) and recover a Godly orientation to our lives.[27] Willard includes chastity, secrecy (practicing good deeds without making them known), and sacrifice (forsaking our need for security) in this category. Disciplines of engagement, by contrast, help counteract sins of omission, moving us to action. Willard notes that the practices of abstinence and engagement counterbalance each other. These are as follows:

- Disciplines of Abstinence: solitude, silence, fasting, simplicity/frugality, chastity, secrecy, sacrifice
- Disciplines of Engagement: study, worship, celebration, service, prayer, fellowship, confession, submission

Other specific spiritual practices not explicitly mentioned by Foster and Willard include hospitality, Sabbath-keeping, retreats, pilgrimages,

27. Willard, *Spirit of the Disciplines*, 156–92.

small groups, tithing, journaling, bodily exercise, testimony, healing, dying well, spiritual resistance, justice, and reconciliation. The concept and practice of spiritual disciplines can be quite broad and there is overlap between them. Prayer is both inward and outward, both solitary and communal; it can involve both abstinence and engagement. Prayer can lead us to fast, confession can free us to worship; all lead to celebration.[28] Not every act is necessarily a discipline (e.g., celebration, service) but can incidentally strengthen our faith. Worship and fellowship are both disciplines and natural parts of the Christian life. There is much overlap between spiritual disciplines and Christian piety; perhaps differences can be discerned on the basis of intent, motivation, and expression.

Although meant for everyone, not just the "spiritual elite," practicing spiritual disciplines can be challenging. They are not a quick fix or technique, and cannot be done simply when we feel like it.[29] (However, typically, the more we practice disciplines, the more we will feel like practicing them, and the easier it will become.) Some people may feel more called to certain practices than others and/or find some more challenging than others. There is no set structure or amount of time required for the exercise of spiritual disciplines. Willard suggests that we "engage in them conscientiously and creatively and adapt them to our individual needs, time, and place."[30] There are many different forms of worship; some people may fast completely, others limit themselves to vegetables (Dan 1:12). In fact, as recommended for most aspects of life, a range of activities is important. What is essential is intentionality, our desire to be faithful followers of Jesus.

Many spiritual disciplines are countercultural—simplicity, confession, and justice are not common in our contemporary Western world. Jonathan Wilson-Hartgrove suggests a practice that is in direct response to our constantly changing and high-speed world.[31] In his book, *Wisdom of Stability,* he stresses the importance of rootedness, purposeful community-building and staying in one place, despite our highly mobile world. Equally needed is the cultivation of steadfastness of the heart. Stability is one way to counter the splintering that characterizes much of life. As per the theme of this book, spiritual practices not only draw us toward Christ, but lead us outward to bring his light and life to the world.

28. Hence the title of Foster's book; see *Celebration of Discipline*, 201.
29. E.g., Willard, *Spirit of the Disciplines*, 70.
30. Willard, *Spirit of the Disciplines*, 191.
31. Wilson-Hartgrove, *Wisdom of Stability*.

In sum, there are many reasons for Christians to practice spiritual disciplines. First, and most importantly, they help us become more aware of God. It is only in stillness that we can hear the "sound of sheer silence" (1 Kgs 19:12).[32] It is only through intention that we can sit at the feet of Jesus (Luke 10:39). It is only by studying the Bible, seeking spiritual guidance, and submitting to servant leaders that we can learn to live faithful, godly lives.

Second, disciplines also help us to be more aware of ourselves. They help us recognize and overcome the habits that enslave us (Rom 3, 7).[33] Through silence, prayer, study, and submission, our eyes can be opened to the dangers of worldly emptiness and the temptations to fill ourselves with something other than God. Mission consultants Alan Roxburgh and Fred Romanuk summarize this well: "The practices help us discern how we are shaped by habits that deform Christian life . . . [they] help us unmask our captivity while forming us."[34]

Third, it is through this combination of self- and God-awareness that spiritual formation thrives. As Foster states, disciplines "allow us to place ourselves before God so that he can transform us."[35] It is in cultivating Christlikeness, in various disciplinary ways, that we fix our attention on Christ: simply put, we worship him. Worship reveals and liberates us from idolatry, from offering worship—deliberately or not—to objects and entities that do not deserve it.

Finally, spiritual practices, even those that occur when we are alone, build Christian community. Through the disciplines we can relearn the largely forgotten habits "developed over the centuries that assist in cultivating Christian identity."[36] Our faith has a strong foundation in Christ and the church. Finally, spiritual disciplines free us and prepare us to participate in God-given and God-oriented mission.

---

32. Solitude and silence open us to the divine presence in a way that goes beyond usual human effort, and contrasts to secular "self-help" exercises; Barton, *Invitation to Solitude*, esp. 31.

33. E.g., Foster, *Celebration of Discipline*, 4–6.

34. Roxburgh and Romanuk, *Missional Leader*, 153.

35. Foster, *Celebration of Discipline*, 7, see also 4–6.

36. Roxburgh and Romanuk, *Missional Leader*, 153.

The Movements of Mission

I have attended many church events during which missionaries, on furlough from exotic locales, tell stories of dramatic conversions and healings, accompanied by exotic images projected onto a large screen. To be honest, I'm usually partly fascinated and partly skeptical. However, the Christian practice and conception of mission have changed in the past few decades.[37] We now take a broader view, incorporating spirituality, theology, cultural sensitivity, and ecological awareness. We recognize the nuances and multidimensional nature of mission and that it can be local as well as global.

The term originates with the Latin *missio*, meaning to be ejected or pushed out, and is usually understood as God's sending of us into the world to "make disciples of all nations" (Matt 28:19). It is "all that God is doing in his great purpose for the whole of creation and all that he calls us to do in cooperation with that purpose."[38] Biblical metaphors for mission include agricultural (Matt 9:37), fishing (Matt 4:19), architectural (1 Cor 3:9–15), and athletic (1 Cor 9:24–27).[39] There is always a sense of activity, of movement. This can be both temporal and spatial—toward a new future and a new horizon.[40] Motion is also centripetal (inward, recognizing God as the author of mission, the one in whom we abide) and centrifugal (outward, recognizing that God sends us into the world). Mission occurs somewhere between the very particular history of Jesus and God's universal goal of inaugurating and completing his kingdom. We live in the "movement from Pentecost to Christ's return, from creation to new creation, from Jerusalem to the ends of the earth, to the new Jerusalem."[41] God's mission also requires us to understand our neighbors, to be informed about our post-Christian, postmodern culture, and to graciously engage and confront it when necessary.[42]

---

37. For overviews see Bosch, *Transforming Mission;* Bauckham, *Bible and Mission*; Ott et al., *Theology of Mission*. David Bosch suggests six essential components of Western missiology: ecological concerns, countercultural values and practices, ecumenical focus, contextualization, focus on the ministry of the laity, and flowing from a worshiping community; *Believing in the Future*, 55–59.

38. Wright, *Mission of God's People*, 24.

39. E.g., Muck and Adeney, *Christianity Encountering*, 303–26.

40. Bauckham, *Bible and Mission*, 13–26, 72–79; the new center is "everywhere and nowhere."

41. Ott et al., *Theology of Mission*, 52, see also 21–41.

42. E.g., Chevalier, "Mission and Spirituality."

Missiology is tied to ecclesiology. The church has a mission but, perhaps more importantly, the mission of Christ creates the church.[43] Our identity is formed through understanding our role in God's purpose for the world. As missiologist Christopher Wright states: "Mission was not made for the church; the church was made for mission—God's mission."[44] This may seem obvious but is something that easily becomes peripheral. The mission of God—*missio Dei*—requires us to live out the gospel of Christ and recognize the abiding presence of the Holy Spirit.

Although the Spirit is not confined to the church, his presence is especially tied to the community of Christ. Indeed, we are "the dwelling place of God" (Eph 2:22), and the reason we are "built into a spiritual house" is to be "a holy priesthood" and "proclaim the mighty acts" of God (1 Pet 2:5, 9). We are called to be witnesses of God's saving presence both overtly and covertly.[45] And of course, the closer we are to the Lord (through practicing spiritual disciplines!) the more effective our Christian witness will be. Again, we see the dialectic of inner and outer rhythms.

In sum, the movements of mission are manifold. We look back in understanding the history of God's people, and forward toward the culmination of God's kingdom. We look near to our own Christian communities and neighborhoods, and far toward the nations. We look outward toward others, discerning their needs, and inward at ourselves, discovering our own motivations. And we look everywhere in every time toward the author of our faith. Mission and spirituality are intertwined.

The Rhythms of Spiritual Disciplines and Mission

It is common for Christian youth to seek discernment about God's calling for their lives. However, Christopher Wright suggests that instead of asking "what kind of mission God has for *me*," we should ask "what kind of me God wants for *his* mission."[46] As we have seen, Scripture teaches

---

43. Goheen, *Church and Its Vocation*, 5; following Moltmann, *Church in the Power of the Spirit*.

44. Wright, *Mission of God*, 62. Roxburgh and Romanuk similarly note that mission is "God's purpose in and for the whole of creation"; the church "has been called into life to be both the means of this mission and a foretaste of where God is inviting all of creation to go"; *Missional Leader*, xv.

45. For an in-depth theological treatment of mediating divine presence, see Wright, *Providence Made Flesh*.

46. Wright, *Mission of God*, 534.

that inner spiritual practices and outer ministry activities are equally important. Indeed, it could be argued that the entire Bible is simultaneously a spiritual and a missional endeavor.[47]

This overlap between mission and spirituality is a common theme in recent missiological studies, perhaps related to the increased interest in pneumatology in the past few decades.[48] In 2011 the World Council of Churches formed a working group on the pneumatological foundations of mission. Participants note that this concept is biblically based; we are dependent on the Holy Spirit, our companion and counselor, and spiritual discernment is important. A trinitarian theology of mission emphasizes "the pneumatological character of God's saving presence."[49] We share the gospel of Christ through the power of the Spirit and through bearing God's image and mediating his presence.

Christian spirituality is rooted in a missionary God; therefore, it is inherently missionary. We join in God's mission as we live our Christian lives and practice spiritual disciplines. Spirituality motivates and sustains mission, although we may not always be aware of this. In spiritual formation, we align our spirits with God's Spirit; in mission, we align our activity with the tasks of God. The closer we are to the Lord, the better we can feel his love and concern for the world. Consequently, Christian spirituality and mission can be viewed as virtually synonymous.[50] Spiritual disciplines are not just about what we can do, but about what God is already doing (recall the tension between divine initiative and human responsibility).

Classic discussions of spiritual disciplines often neglect both the larger story of the mission of God and his people, and the cultural contexts in which we practice these disciplines. Both spirituality and mission are dynamic processes, requiring continual reflection and reinterpretation through an ongoing relationship with the indwelling Spirit. It can be challenging to live distinctively and deliberately as citizens of God's kingdom, cultivating practices that engage and counter-engage the values and structures of Western culture. Therefore, spiritual disciplines need to be missionally practicable.

---

47. Wright, *Mission of God*, 5–28.

48. Although there is tension in this relationship and disagreement on how they are connected; e.g., Chevalier, "Mission and Spirituality"; Helland and Hjalmarson. *Missional Spirituality*.

49. World Council of Churches, "Companions in the Spirit," 43.

50. Suderman, *Calloused Hands*, esp. 8.

One helpful approach is that of evangelical scholar David Fitch. He suggests seven disciplines, somewhat different from the classic ones, to help us both reimagine the church and better engage the world. These practices shape the church for mission. They are ways to reflect God's faithful presence that are not constrained by the organized church. Rather, they move from the church to beyond, and are particularly needed in our contemporary hungry, lonely, antagonistic, and splintered world. Fitch's spiritual practices are:[51]

- the Lord's Table—sharing a meal and tending to Christ's presence;
- reconciliation—seeking forgiveness, inclusion, and solidarity; opening space for the Spirit to work;
- proclaiming the gospel—with humility, in various places and manners, to make way for the kingdom of God;
- being with the "least of these"—by enacting Christ's presence in the world;
- being with children—by including them in all aspects of church, as they make Christ's presence real to us;
- the fivefold gifting (apostles, prophets, evangelists, pastors, teachers; Eph 4:8)—as mutual and interdependent, practicing and revealing divine presence according to need; and
- kingdom prayer—as a way to reorder the world and join, with submission, in God's work.

Fitch's disciplines, along with the classic ones, offer approaches to spirituality and mission. As will become apparent, there is no limit to how this is practiced in our Christian lives, especially when interpreted broadly. In the chapters following, we will read about both lived examples and fresh perspectives on the rhythms of mission and spiritual disciplines. The contributors to this volume are diverse in their experience and writing style: some are more academic, reflective; others more personal. All speak to the spiritual poverty of our culture, the need for us to sing in a countercultural manner, and the intertwining of spiritual disciplines and mission.

First, Michael Gorman, with vivid examples and insightful biblical exegesis, addresses the "lure of imperial religion and the missional power of the cross." Because of the prevalence of nationalism, which is idolatrous, it

51. Fitch, *Faithful Presence*.

is necessary for Christian communities to be countercultural. We are called to abstain from worldly worship and instead follow Christ in taking up our cross, dying to ourselves and serving others. This "discipline of cruciformity" requires us to live "cross-shaped" lives. Other spiritual disciplines, such as prayer, fasting, and hospitality are grounded in Christ's work on the cross. Gorman deepens our insight into why we practice spiritual disciplines and engage in missional activities. The purpose and the content of our songs are important—always reflecting submission to Christ.

In chapter 2, Dave Witt shares some of his experience working with the TrueCity network of churches, specifically its multi-church missional discipleship program. He notes that Christians are called to join God in his mission to reconcile all things to himself—deepening our relationships with him, fellow believers, and the cities where we live. Ministry is much more than mere programs. But, without proper discipleship practices, those involved are prone to burnout. Mission occurs in the context of discipleship and vice versa. Discipleship employs spiritual disciplines and is best done in community. Witt engages with Fitch's church disciplines, noting the importance of communal practices such as discernment. His chapter provides context for mission and its prerequisite spiritual preparation—they involve intentional rhythms of inward and outward focus.

The next two chapters examine two of Foster's classic disciplines: prayer and study. Michael Knowles unpacks key biblical passages on prayer and points out that it not only has a mission but is itself a mission. Through this inward discipline we join with Jesus in asking for God's will to be done and thus participate in God's mission. We should always listen spiritually before speaking and acting missionally. Like Witt and Gorman, Knowles addresses the "why" of a particular spiritual discipline, prayer, more than the "how." There is always an element of mystery and, with respect to prayer, mission and spiritual practice are almost inseparable.

Seán McGuire, in his study of study, also focuses on reasons and context rather than method. Immersing oneself in the Bible is a spiritual foundation of mission. Through this spiritual practice, we come closer to loving God with all our minds and learn how to live as kingdom citizens. We study Scripture—concentrating and comprehending—not only to learn about the triune God but also to know him better. However, this is never simply a private endeavor: both the written and incarnate Word need to be articulated, reflected in our actions, and put into practice. Bible study draws us closer to God so that our mission aligns with his—such are the rhythms of spiritual and missional practice.

In chapter 5, I suggest that the spiritual and psychological practice of mindfulness is a type of spiritual discipline, related to contemplative prayer, that can increase our openness to mission moments. Instead of following our culture of noise and busyness, we can work on being fully present in each moment of our day—present to Christ and present to those who need his presence. Thus, our ministry can be more mindful and better aligned with the *missio Dei*. Mission and mindfulness intertwine.

The final three chapters provide some practical examples of the rhythms of mission and spiritual discipline. Aaron Smith describes his experience as a missionary in the Philippines and argues that neighborhood engagement is a spiritual discipline, one that complements the classic ones. Moving to an area, becoming part of the community, inviting people for dinner—this is how we can engage and show love for our neighbors. And we love God by loving our neighbors, whose names and faces we know. Smith notes the reciprocal relationship between ministry and spiritual disciplines, especially prayer and study. These practices remind us of the need to practice hospitality, and when we are engaged with our neighbors we are reminded to pray and know specifically what to pray about. Love and action are intertwined. Both enable our own spiritual transformation.

In chapter 7, Jill Weber shares her experience of "loitering with intention" in a prayer truck in inner city Hamilton. She engages the spiritual disciplines of prayer and hospitality, and notes the importance of creating space and time for God to work, even though it is often inconvenient for us. We need to overcome our own preoccupations, protections, and prejudices in order to truly see and be with those we encounter. Learning to see through Jesus's eyes leads to worship. Like Smith, Weber implicitly notes the connection between the spiritual practice of discerning the presence and action of God and joining him in his mission.

In the next chapter, songwriter Peter Tigchelaar talks about his involvement with the March for Jesus movement as well as other ministries in the city of Hamilton. He notes the importance of the biblical concept of the house of the Lord, the place where his glory dwells, in contrast to false houses that are self-serving. Christians are called to mediate God's presence and, by doing so, we can redeem people and places. Tigchelaar intertwines his stories and metaphors with a song that speaks about "chimes of redemption" and the "body of love." As in the previous chapter, discerning divine presence is essential, and can occur simultaneously with the missional bearing of this presence.

Finally, I offer a brief conclusion that reviews and reconnects the chapters to concepts discussed in this introduction, as well as sharing some challenges for all who are called to sing into splintered spaces.

No matter what metaphors we use, what specific practices we prefer, or what specific ministries we are active in, there are always rhythms in our Christian lives. And these occur within the larger rhythms of divine initiative and human responsibility. As we engage with our world as participants in God's work and ambassadors of his kingdom, we continually and consciously move inward and outward, following the model and teachings of Jesus, in obedience to divine calling. We sing and dance in worship, then are quiet in contemplation. We sing good news into the splintered spaces of contemporary culture. We dance out into our world. We dance in compassionate action. In authentic Christian living, we need rhythms of resting and responding, listening and leading, praying and proclaiming. We need both singing and silence, both feasting and fasting, both socialization and solitude.

> Look for the ancient paths where the good way lies, and sing and dance in them. (Jer 6:16, paraphrased)

Bibliography

Barton, Ruth Haley. *Invitation to Solitude and Silence: Experiencing God's Transforming Presence*. 2nd ed. Downers Grove, IL: Intervarsity, 2010.

———. *Sacred Rhythms: Arranging Our Lives for Spiritual Transformation*. Downers Grove, IL: InterVarsity, 2006.

Bauckham, Richard. *Bible and Mission: Christian Witness in a Postmodern World*. Grand Rapids: Baker, 2003.

Block, Peter, et al. *An Other Kingdom: Departing the Consumer Culture*. New York: Wiley, 2016.

Bosch, David J. *Believing in the Future: Toward a Missiology of Western Culture*. Valley Forge, PA: Trinity, 1995.

———. *Transforming Mission: Paradigm Shifts in Theology of Mission*. Maryknoll, NY: Orbis, 1991.

Carson, D. A. "Spiritual Disciplines." *Themelios* 36.3 (2011). https://www.thegospelcoalition.org/themelios/article/spiritual-disciplines/.

Chevalier, Laura A. "Mission and Spirituality: Ecumenical Convergence and Creative Tensions in a New Millennium." *Missiology: An International Review* 45.3 (2017) 322–35.

Coakley, Sarah. "Introduction." In *Faith, Rationality and the Passions*, edited by Sarah Coakley, 1–12. Chichester, Sussex: Wiley-Blackwell, 2012.
Crouch, Andy. *The Tech-Wise Family: Everyday Steps for Putting Technology in Its Proper Place*. Grand Rapids: Baker, 2017.
Fitch, David E. *Faithful Presence: Seven Disciplines that Shape the Church for Mission*. Downers Grove, IL: Intervarsity, 2016.
Foster, Richard J. *Celebration of Discipline: The Path to Spiritual Growth*. 3rd ed. New York: HarperOne, 1998.
———. *Freedom of Simplicity*. New York: HarperCollins, 1981.
Friedman, Meyer, and Ray Rosenman. *Type A Behavior and Your Heart*. New York: Alfred Knopf, 1974.
Gay, Craig M. *Modern Technology and the Human Future: A Christian Appraisal*. Downers Grove, IL: IVP Academic, 2018.
Goheen, Michael. *The Church and Its Vocation: Lesslie Newbigin's Missionary Ecclesiology*. Grand Rapids: Baker Academic, 2018.
Helland, Roger, and Leornard Hjalmarson. *Missional Spirituality: Embodying God's Love from the Inside Out*. Downers Grove, IL: IVP, 2011.
Howard, Evan B. *The Brazos Introduction to Christian Spirituality*. Grand Rapids: Brazos, 2008.
Jensen, L. Paul. *Subversive Spirituality: Transforming Mission through the Collapse of Space and Time*. Eugene, OR: Pickwick, 2009.
Kinnaman, David, and Aly Hawkins. *You Lost Me: Why Young Christians Are Leaving Church . . . and Rethinking Faith*. Grand Rapids: Baker, 2016.
Lasch, Christopher. *Culture of Narcissism: American Life in an Age of Diminishing Expectations*. New York: Norton, 1979.
May, Gerald G. *Addiction and Grace*. San Francisco: HarperCollins, 1988.
McGilchrist, Iain. *The Master and His Emissary: The Divided Brain and the Making of the Western World*. New Haven, CT: Yale University Press, 2009.
McGrath, Alister E. *Christian Spirituality: An Introduction*. Oxford: Blackwell, 1999.
McLaren, Brian. *Finding Our Way Again: The Return of the Ancient Practices*. Nashville: Thomas Nelson, 2010.
Middleton, J. Richard, and Brian J. Walsh. *Truth Is Stranger than It Used to Be: Biblical Faith in a Postmodern Age*. Downers Grove, IL: Intervarsity, 1995.
Muck, Terry, and Frances S. Adeney. *Christianity Encountering World Religions: The Practice of Mission in the Twenty-First Century*. Grand Rapids: Baker Academic, 2009
Ott, Craig, et al. *Encountering Theology of Mission: Biblical Foundations, Historical Developments and Contemporary Issues*. Grand Rapids: Baker, 2010.
Pearcey, Nancy R. *Total Truth: Liberating Christianity from Its Cultural Captivity*. Wheaton, IL: Crossway, 2004.
Putman, Robert D. *Bowling Alone: The Collapse and Revival of American Community*. New York: Simon & Schuster, 2001.
Roxburgh, Alan, and Fred Romanuk. *The Missional Leader: Equipping Your Church to Reach a Changing World*. San Francisco: Jossey-Bass, 2006.
Smith, Robert, Jr. "The Spiritual Wisdom of the African American Tradition." In *For All the Saints: Evangelical Theology and Christian Spirituality*, edited by Timothy George and Alister McGrath, 165–74. Louisville: Westminster John Knox, 2003
Strasburger, Jordan, et al. "Health Effects of Media on Children and Adolescents." *Pediatrics* 135.4 (2010) 756–67.

Suderman R. J. *Calloused Hands, Courageous Souls: Holistic Spirituality of Development and Mission*. Monrovia, CA: MARC, 1998.
TrueCity. "TrueCity," 2021. https://www.truecity.ca/.
Webber, Robert E. *The Divine Embrace: Recovering the Passionate Spiritual Life*. Grand Rapids: Baker, 2006.
Willard, Dallas. *The Spirit of the Disciplines: Understanding How God Changes Lives*. San Francisco: Harper & Row, 1988.
Wilson, Jonathan R. *Living Faithfully in a Fragmented World: From "After Virtue" to the New Monasticism*. 2nd ed. Eugene, OR: Wipf & Stock, 2010.
Wilson-Hartgrove, Jonathan. *The Wisdom of Stability: Rooting Faith in a Mobile Culture*. Brewster, MA: Paraclete, 2010.
World Council of Churches. "Companions in the Spirit—Companions in Mission: Reflections on Mission and Spirituality." *International Review of Mission* 101.1 (2012) 43–60.
Wright, Christopher J. H. *The Mission of God: Unlocking the Bible's Grand Narrative*. Downers Grove, IL: IVP Academic, 2006.
———. *The Mission of God's People: A Biblical Theology of the Church's Mission*. Grand Rapids: Zondervan, 2010.
Wright, Terry J. *Providence Made Flesh: Divine Presence as a Framework for a Theology of Providence*. Eugene, OR: Wipf & Stock, 2009.

Chapter 1

The Discipline of Cruciformity

Civil Religion and the Missional Power of the Cross

 MICHAEL J. GORMAN

A FRIEND OF MINE became a pastor at about the age of forty. The appointment system in the United Methodist church means that pastors start new ministry assignments each year on July 1. Therefore, in the US, their first Sunday in a new church is on or around Independence Day, the Fourth of July: the most patriotic celebration of the American year. It is often a Sunday for patriotic "hymns" and sermons, and sometimes even flag waving and reciting the Pledge of Allegiance. However, these are not true Christian worship activities but are actually misguided practices of civil religion, or Christian nationalism.[1]

On the Saturday morning before his first service with his first congregation, my friend met with the church's lay leader, who had prepared a PowerPoint presentation for the service. It included photos of flags and the texts of patriotic songs. Gently, but with conviction, my friend said to the lay leader, "I appreciate your hard work, but I'm wondering if we could change the PowerPoint. I have no problem with people celebrating their country after church, but could we just focus on Jesus during church?" The lay leader did not even pause to think before responding, "You are the pastor. I will change the slides"—and he did. Thus began a long, deep friendship between my pastor-friend and the lay leader, as well as the entire church.

---

1. For the purposes of this essay, I will consider the terms "civil religion" and "Christian nationalism" to be synonyms.

Spiritual disciplines are sometimes characterized as disciplines of abstinence and disciplines of engagement.[2] In fact, these two types of disciplines sometimes—or perhaps regularly—overlap. My pastor friend asked the lay leader to abstain from one form of worship to engage in another. Consider the words of Peter and the other apostles: "We must obey God rather than any human authority" (Acts 5:29). Obeying God here involves disobeying authorities, which is certainly a form of abstinence. Think also of Paul's oft-quoted words in Romans: "Do not be conformed to this world [literally "this age"], but be transformed by the renewing of your minds, so that you may discern what is the will of God—what is good and acceptable and perfect" (Rom 12:2). Being transformed in order to discern God's will is itself a form of engagement in multiple ways, but it obviously involves a form of *dis*engagement, or abstinence, specifically from the prevailing worldview or social imaginary. Indeed, some have said that Rom 12:2 points to the reality that all Christian education, or formation, involves both unlearning and relearning.

We do not have to look far in Scripture for other examples of what we might call *engaged abstinence* or, even better, *abstinent engagement*. Jesus himself said, "No one can serve two masters; for a slave will either hate the one and love the other, or be devoted to the one and despise the other. You cannot serve God and wealth [Mammon]" (Matt 6:24; cf. Luke 16:13). He also made it clear that discipleship could sometimes require difficult decisions about priorities, resulting in abstinence for the sake of engagement:

> As they were going along the road, someone said to him, "I will follow you wherever you go." And Jesus said to him, "Foxes have holes, and birds of the air have nests; but the Son of Man has nowhere to lay his head." To another he said, "Follow me." But he said, "Lord, first let me go and bury my father." But Jesus said to him, "Let the dead bury their own dead; but as for you, go and proclaim the kingdom of God." (Luke 9:57–60; cf. Matt 8:18–22)

These words from Jesus also make it clear that abstinent engagement is, or is at least sometimes, *missional* in character.

The claim of this chapter is that the spiritual discipline of individual and corporate cruciformity—deliberately chosen cross-shaped existence in Christ—is a form of abstinent engagement that is also missional in nature. That is what my pastor friend was practicing, and what he was inviting his church to practice with him. Embracing the cross and the

---

2. E.g., Willard, *Spirit of the Disciplines*, 156–92; *Divine Conspiracy*, 417–18.

Crucified—the one Roman imperial powers put to death because they saw him as a threat to the status quo—is also unavoidably political. This does not mean it adheres to a specific political party or political agenda. Rather, because Jesus was a challenge to the status quo, following him will also often be a challenge to the powers-that-be.

Think, for instance, of what happened when Paul and his colleagues preached the Gospel in places like Philippi and Thessaloniki in ancient Greece (Acts 16:6—17:9). The Gospel naturally challenged the reigning economic, social, and political status quo, so the Pauline team was accused of "disturbing our city . . . advocating customs that are not lawful for us as Romans to adopt or observe" (Acts 16:20–21). They were also charged with "turning the world upside down" and "acting contrary to the decrees of the emperor, saying that there is another king named Jesus" (Acts 17:6–7). As a result, they endured the anger of both mobs and public officials: they were attacked, flogged, and jailed (Acts 16:20–24; 17:5–9). Paul and his coworkers—as well as those transformed by their ministry—were living the Gospel of Christ crucified, not merely speaking about it. Cruciformity is missional, specifically evangelistic, because it offers an alternative way of life to that prescribed by the normal politics of power and the religious entities that underwrite it.

We begin with a consideration of civil religion as a religion of power, expressed especially in certain kinds of liturgies, and to the attraction of such religion. We then turn to a description of the discipline of cruciformity and to the power of the cross to reshape our understanding of religion, God, and power itself, arguing that this discipline is a form of evangelization. In light of this proposal, we next consider one popular (at least in some circles) traditional hymn and one popular example of contemporary "worship music" to see how they should be understood and sung as part of a counter-liturgy, a corporate spiritual discipline, of evangelistic abstinent engagement.

Readers will keep in mind that I write from the context of the United States during and immediately following the presidency of Donald Trump, which certainly affects my understanding of all that I propose. At the same time, I have expressed similar sentiments during other US presidencies, and the specific incidents I mention below are hardly outliers in the story of Christianity in the United States, or in the West more generally.[3]

---

3. The marked increase in Christian nationalism in the US, with special reference to the Trump era, is documented and interpreted by Whitehead and Perry, *Taking America*.

The Lure of Civil Religion/Christian Nationalism

I illustrate the lure of civil religion with two additional anecdotes, both involving allegedly sacred music. Christians will remember that when we sing, we pray twice.[4]

"Make America Great Again"

On July 1, 2017, just before the first US Independence Day of Donald Trump's presidency, the First Baptist Church choir of Dallas, Texas, assisted by other choirs, performed at a "Celebrate Freedom Rally" at the John F. Kennedy Center for the Performing Arts in Washington, DC. The pastor of First Baptist, Robert Jeffress, was an ardent Trump supporter. The song, which resulted in an approving tweet from Trump, was called "Make America Great Again," from Trump's campaign slogan.[5] It was composed by the church's former minister of music and was for a time included in the Christian Copyright Licensing International (CCLI) database, the bank of songs that churches can legally reproduce and use if they have a CCLI license. The main words of the "hymn" are found in the title, words that are repeated throughout each verse and account for nearly half the song's text. In addition, there are references to common American themes and symbols, such as freedom, blessing, unity, vision, and the eagle.

Reactions to this performance ranged across the spectrum, from strong support to strong denunciation. What the song and its performance reveal—the church choir sang with an enormous American flag hanging behind them—is the blending of patriotism, even nationalism, and some form of Christian faith. It must be said, however, that there is very little explicitly religious, much less Christian, about the text. Yet even a casual listener will hear religious overtones, and a careful hearer or reader will connect the text with the language of American "Manifest Destiny," which is also, for many, religious or quasi-religious language.

It is especially the obviously religious character of the composer, the singers, and the church's pastor that makes the song into a hymn, a form of praise. Their creating and performing the song should be seen as an act

---

4. Although I have been told there was some music associated with people who witnessed or participated in the storming of the US Capitol on January 6, 2021, I am resisting the temptation to relate that unique incident in favor of more "ordinary" ones.

5. See the news story at Thomsen, "Church Choir Sings."

not only of praise, but also of evangelism—of proclaiming "good news." More specifically, it is—in the tradition of revivalism—a hymn of invitation. This good news, however, has nothing to do with Jesus Christ, and the invitation is not to follow him. It is an invitation, ironically, to help perfect an imperfect, indeed a "fallen," nation that is (allegedly) uniquely blessed and the ongoing source, potentially, of divine blessing. What is needed, according to the song, is a revival.

One could argue that "Make America Great Again" is less religious than, say, "God Bless America," or that it is not really meant to make the US into an idol because it does not explicitly offer praise to the country as an alternative to worshiping the triune God revealed in the crucified and resurrected Jesus. But such arguments miss the main point: the nationalistic, political message of a president has usurped the Gospel of Jesus Christ as the substance of what these (supposedly Christian) people proclaim and invite others to proclaim. Rather than singing the Christian Gospel "to a splintered world that desperately needs a new song"—as Janet Warren puts it in the introduction to this book—civil religion offers us an old, tired, and misguided song that ultimately produces death rather than life.

"Please Stand for the National Anthem"

For more than a half-century, many sporting events in the United States have begun with the singing of the national anthem, for which it is expected that all attendees, including players, stand and face the US flag. As a form of protest—usually of injustice—some Americans, including members of professional sports teams, have refused to stand. In the autumn of 2017, this came to a head, as certain prominent football players knelt during the national anthem as a form of protest, particularly against ongoing violence against African Americans.

We do not need to get bogged down in the details, but the reaction from many everyday sports fans to the President of the United States was one of disdain for these players. Astute Christian observers of American culture, however, identify this reaction as the logical outcome of the way that sports, especially American football, have become forms of civil religion, in which sacred devotion to the country, its flag, its anthem, and its military heroes is expected to be on full display by all in attendance. The words of Christian philosopher James Smith, written for the American holiday of Thanksgiving (and football), are insightful and worth quoting at length:

> Thanksgiving has always been one of the high holy days of American civil religion. . . . Our Thanksgiving traditions reflect the country's mix of secularization and religious fervor—what theologian William Cavanaugh calls "migrations of the holy." . . . In a secular age, our religious impulses aren't diminished; they just find new devotions: consumption, the self, the nation. Now, the NFL [National Football League]—in all its popularity and current controversy—sets the script for our Thanksgiving Day litany. It gives us something to worship. . . . The pomp and fandom in NFL stadiums across the country display their own rituals—and reveal how our gratitude has shifted [away from God]. We give thanks to the military, tout our freedoms and celebrate the exceptional blessings of "this great country." The military serves as the tangible, almost sacramental, embodiment of the nation's mythology. . . . You know you've entered a temple when disagreement is treated as sacrilege. *The animosity directed toward NFL players kneeling at the anthem, protesting police brutality and structural racism, is the sort of acrimony we reserve for infidels.* . . . This is how stadiums became temples of nationalism. When the Constitution functions like Scripture, and the pledge serves as our creed, and the flag is revered like the cross, and the national anthem becomes our hymn, and the hand over heart is a sacred expression like the sign of the cross, then a swelling patriotism becomes our religion and dissenters are heretics.[6]

One might observe that, in light of the Black Lives Matter movement as well as other reactions to the many killings of Black Americans, such protests are now acceptable in the United States. This is a fair point, but I would suggest that even if certain forms of protest are and remain part of American life, the realities of nationalism and its association with sports have not disappeared and will not disappear in the future; they are engrained in the American sports culture.

Civil Religion

These incidents in the life of the United States—for which there are parallel, analogous incidents elsewhere—are manifestations of fervent civil religion, which may be defined as follows:

---

6. Smith, "NFL's Thanksgiving Games" (emphasis added).

The attribution of sacred status to secular power (normally the state and/or its head) as the source of divine blessing, requiring devotion and allegiance of heart, mind, and body to the sacred-secular power and its values, all expressed in various narratives, other texts, rituals, and media that reinforce both the secular power's sacred status and the beneficiaries' sacred duty of devotion and allegiance, even to the point of death.[7]

This definition of civil religion implies that it has three major dimensions:

1. *Ideology/theology*: the *sacralization of the state*, including: (a) its power, prosperity, and peace; (b) its activities and accomplishments, especially in expansion and war; (c) its guiding myths and values; and (d) its past heroes and current leader(s);

2. *Commitment/practices*: the corollary demand of *solemn devotion and allegiance* to the state as a sacred responsibility (including the willingness to kill and/or die for it) to be *expressed in public rituals*; and

3. *Syncretism*: the *reinterpretation of the culture's dominant religious tradition(s)* to incorporate this sacralization of the state and solemn allegiance to it; the mixing of religious faith and practice with political, nationalistic claims and practices.

The lure of civil religion is that it connects diverse people to a common, even ultimate, cause—their country—as an experience of shared participation in transcendence, which is often thought to be a God-experience. Theologically speaking, this sort of religion is idolatrous, but the profound irony is that many people who practice it think they are actually practicing their own religious faith, whether Christianity, Judaism, or whatever. Various forms of public civil religion permeate American civic and religious discourse and practices—that is, as individual and (especially) corporate "spiritual disciplines."[8] Among these forms are the following sacred rituals and holy days:

---

7. This definition and list of practices are taken from my *Reading Revelation Responsibly*, 46–54.

8. There are numerous books and articles on this topic. One recent analysis is Gardella, *American Civil Religion*, who finds four values at the core of this religion: freedom/liberty, democracy, peace, and tolerance. Gardella, however, is (in my view) too positive toward his topic, and he underestimates the importance of "sacred violence" to American civil religion. For sacred violence as an American sacrament, see Laderman, *American Civil Religion*.

- **Civil rituals made religious**
  - Official days of prayer
  - National feasts/holy days
    - Martin Luther King Day
    - Presidents' Day
    - Memorial Day
    - Independence Day/Fourth of July
    - Veterans Day
    - Thanksgiving
  - State funerals
  - Moments of silence
  - Congressional chaplaincy
  - Prayer at political and civic events
  - Prayer around the flagpole
  - National days of prayer, prayer breakfasts
  - The Pledge of Allegiance, at school or other civic gatherings, to the flag as icon of a nation "under God"
  - The national anthem at sporting events
  - Swearing on the Bible
  - Chaplains' prayers before military combat missions
- **Religious rituals made civil**
  - Pledge of Allegiance in church
  - Recognition of active military or veterans in church at national holidays
  - Prayers for "those serving our country," "the troops," and especially "our troops" in church
  - Sermons and children's sermons on patriotic themes
  - Use of patriotic music in worship
  - Religious events on national holidays
  - Religious gatherings in times of national crisis

In civil religion that permeates a nation with great, even unsurpassed, political, military, and economic power, we have the religion of imperial power. We do not need to formally identify a country as an empire to use such a description. Nor do we need to call Jesus or Paul explicitly anti- or counter-imperial to say that the Christian Gospel is itself the antithesis of the civil religion of power that is expressed in the rituals noted above. My pastor friend whose story is told at the start of this chapter understood this clearly, and stated it graciously.

Roman Civil Religion

Rome had its own form of civil religion, its own gospel, or good news (Greek *euangelion/euangelia*, from which we get words like "evangelism"). An inscription from 9 BC, found at several places around the Empire, speaks of the "savior" Augustus, whom "providence" sent to end war and establish peace:

> [S]ince Caesar when revealed [*epiphanein*] surpassed the hopes of all who had anticipated the good news [*euangelia*], not only going beyond the benefits of those who had preceded him, but rather leaving no hope of surpassing him for those who will come, because of him the birthday of God began good news [*euangelia*] for the world.[9]

Similar in sentiment are the words of Horace, in a poem (*Carmen saeculare*) from 17 BC written for games—public liturgies—in honor of Augustus: "Now good faith, and peace, and honor, and modesty ancient, and virtue long-abandoned, do dare to return, and blessed Plenty appears, her horn quite full."[10] In other words, someone is about to make the Empire great again.

Both Jesus and Paul proclaimed, in word and deed, a message that offered alternative good news to this "fake news," thereby challenging the political, military, and economic power of Rome, its deceived and deceiving leaders, and its devoted—but also deceived—followers.[11] For both Jesus and his apostle to the nations, the cross was the ironic antithesis to

---

9. Translation from Elliott and Reasoner, *Documents and Images*, 35.

10. Translation by Neil Elliott in Elliott and Reasoner, *Documents and Images*, 3.

11. The most famous fake news in the US during the time in which I write is also called "the big lie": the claim that the 2020 US presidential election was rigged and/or stolen and that Donald Trump actually won that election.

civil religion, the true presence and power of God in the world—the actual source of peace and blessing.

The Cross of the Lord and His Disciples

There are many distinctive aspects of Christian faith, but few are as counterintuitive, controversial, and yet central as the cross of Jesus Christ. It was Paul who told the Corinthians that he "decided to know nothing among you except Jesus Christ, that is, Jesus Christ crucified" (1 Cor 2:2, my translation) and that the crucified Messiah was "the power of God and the wisdom of God" (1 Cor 1:24). What Christians sometimes forget, however, is that the cross of this Messiah Jesus is not only the *source* of our salvation, but also its *shape*.

That is, our fundamental spiritual discipline is cruciformity—cross-shaped living.[12] For that reason, all other spiritual disciplines are also in a profound way cruciform.[13] For example, contemplative prayer is a way of opening ourselves to the indwelling Spirit of the crucified and resurrected Jesus. Fasting is a way of abstaining from normal ways of life to take on, more deliberately, the way of the cross. Hospitality is the practice of welcoming others in ways that may require us to put aside our own needs and desires in the service of others, as Jesus did in agreeing to be crucified. Worship is the adoration of the triune God whose power and wisdom are most fully on display in the crucified Messiah (1 Cor 1:18–25; see also Rev 4–5).

Cruciformity, therefore, begins with Jesus himself. As all three Synoptic Gospels report, Jesus called his disciples to take up their cross and follow him (Matt 10:38; Mark 8:34; Luke 9:23), with Luke making explicit the obvious: that this must be done "daily." In the three major predictions of his suffering and crucifixion (his "passion") as narrated by Mark, Jesus calls the disciples to

1. self-denial and suffering in witness to the Gospel (Mark 8:31–38);
2. hospitality to the weak and marginalized, represented by children (Mark 9:31–37); and

---

12. The term *cruciform*, meaning "cross-shaped," comes to spirituality from architecture, where it was and is used to describe churches that are built in the form of a cross.

13. For a brief overview of this discipline, see Gorman, "Cruciformity"; for an extended treatment, see Gorman, *Cruciformity*.

3. service to others rather than domination over them, which is practiced by the "gentiles" (those in power) (Mark 10:32–45).[14]

Dietrich Bonhoeffer understood, and lived, this vocation as perhaps no one else in recent Christian memory: "When Christ calls a person, he bids them come and die."[15]

Furthermore, the Gospel of John (chapter 13) tells us that Jesus washed his disciples' feet as a sort of window into the twofold meaning of his imminent crucifixion: that it was both salvific and exemplary. Disciples, both then and now, are called to wash the feet of others, both within their community and in the world as they go out, sent like Jesus:

> Therefore, since I, the Lord (*kyrios*) and Teacher, have washed your feet, you also ought to wash one another's feet. For I have given you an example: that you also should do as I have done to you. Amen, amen, I tell you, no slave is greater than his or her lord (*kyriou*), nor is a sent one (*apostolos*) greater than the one who sent that person. (John 13:14–16; my translation)

That is, for Jesus's disciples the cruciform practice of washing feet—which is to be taken not only literally but also symbolically to represent self-giving, servant-like love—is both an internal and an external missional spiritual practice. The disciples' participation in Jesus's death means that they will become like their master, who is also their sender. To be apostolic—missional—is to do as Jesus did, wherever the individual or community is, or is sent.

It is interesting and significant that the only occurrence of the word *apostle* (*apostolos*) in John's Gospel occurs in this passage. Cruciform footwashing is hardly a practice of Roman, or any other, imperial politics and civil religion of power. It is, rather, the antithesis of such religion and thus the essence of "uncivil" religion. (By which, of course, I do not mean "impolite" or "disrespectful.") It is the spirituality of reaching out to others in the form of lowliness and weakness: taking on the form of a slave, the kind of person who might actually be expected to wash feet.[16]

---

14. See Gorman, "Cruciformity according to Jesus and Paul," expanded in *Death of the Messiah*.

15. This is a slight alteration from the older, more familiar translation of Bonhoeffer's *Nachfolge* entitled *The Cost of Discipleship*, 89. The new translation, in Bonhoeffer, *Discipleship* (87), is "Whenever Christ calls us, his call leads us to death."

16. In antiquity, washing feet was a necessity. Having water for guests to wash their feet was a practice of hospitality, and slaves, if anyone other than the guests themselves,

Similarly, although the apostle Paul does not use the term disciple or discipleship per se, his spirituality of Spirit-enabled conformity to Christ crucified includes the summons to embody Jesus's threefold call:

1. bearing faithful witness even to the point of suffering (e.g., Phil 1:27–30);
2. identifying with the weak as an expression of God's cruciform wisdom and power (Rom 14:1—15:13; 1 Cor 1:18—2:5; 8:1–13); and
3. lovingly, as a servant, seeking the benefit of others rather than self (e.g., 1 Cor 10:23—11:1; 13:5; Phil 2:1-11, which may echo the foot-washing scene in John 13).

In sum, Paul's spirituality of participation in the death of Christ is congruent with—indeed fundamentally the same as—Jesus's call to cross-shaped discipleship.[17]

This focus on the cross and on a cross-shaped spirituality is not, however, the end of the story, or even the full story. Paradoxically, the discipline of cruciformity is full of life and leads to life. That is, cruciformity is *resurrectional*; it is suffused with the resurrection and is therefore life-giving, in two senses.[18] First, death is the prerequisite for life; second, life comes in the midst of death. Both Jesus and Paul make these points.

Said Jesus: "Very truly [Amen, amen], I tell you, unless a grain of wheat falls into the earth and dies, it remains just a single grain; but if it dies, it bears much fruit. Those who love their life lose it, and those who hate their life in this world will keep it for eternal life. Whoever serves me must follow me, and where I am, there will my servant be also. Whoever serves me, the Father will honor (John 12:24–26)."[19] Jesus's words come at the conclusion of the first half of John's Gospel, as Jesus prepares to announce his own death to the disciples and to call them to participate in it.

Paul offers consistent words about Jesus's death, and his participation in it, in Second Corinthians:

> We are afflicted in every way, but not crushed; perplexed, but not driven to despair; persecuted, but not forsaken; struck down, but

---

washed the guests' feet. See Thomas, *Footwashing*.

17. See further Gorman, "Cruciformity according to Jesus and Paul."
18. See further Gorman, *Participating in Christ*, 53–76.
19. Paul appears to make use of this saying, or at least its general sense, in 1 Cor 15:36.

not destroyed; always carrying in the body the death of Jesus, so that the life of Jesus may also be made visible in our bodies. For while we live, we are always being given up to death for Jesus' sake, so that the life of Jesus may be made visible in our mortal flesh. So death is at work in us, but life in you. But just as we have the same spirit of faith that is in accordance with scripture—"I believed, and so I spoke"—we also believe, and so we speak, because we know that the one who raised the Lord Jesus will raise us also with Jesus, and will bring us with you into his presence. Yes, everything is for your sake, so that grace, as it extends to more and more people, may increase thanksgiving, to the glory of God. So we do not lose heart. Even though our outer nature is wasting away, our inner nature is being renewed day by day. For this slight momentary affliction is preparing us for an eternal weight of glory beyond all measure, because we look not at what can be seen but at what cannot be seen; for what can be seen is temporary, but what cannot be seen is eternal. (2 Cor 4:8–18)

In both of these texts, we see that Jesus's death and our participation in it are both inherently missional.[20] Such participation bears fruit, as Jesus says (see also John 15). The ultimate paradox of the cross is that it brings life; *it is the quintessential act of missional abstinent engagement*. A spirituality of the cross and mission are naturally "intertwined," to recall Janet Warren's insights from her introduction.

The Christian community is called to "abstain" from the so-called life offered by the cult of civil religion, including the alleged power associated with it. It is simultaneously called to practice "death" in the form of Christlike self-sacrificial love. It thereby engages both others and God, and therefore also experiences true life and power.

Life-Giving Evangelism and Singing

In light of these discussions of both civil religion and cruciformity, I want to briefly suggest two aspects of a life-giving spiritual practice of evangelism that emerges from them as an alternative to the "good news" on offer from civil religion.

---

20. Throughout Second Corinthians, Paul's use of "we" sometimes refers first of all to himself and his colleagues in ministry. Yet these texts can, by analogy, apply to all members of the body of Christ because each one has a spiritual gift, participating in the ongoing life and ministry of Christ by the working of the Spirit.

The first aspect is the nature of normal Christian community as evangelistic—when it is resurrectionally cruciform. When individual Christians and the church wash feet, they are bearing *fruit* as they bear *witness* to the cross of our Lord. Footwashing is always contextual; Christian communities must pray for the ability to discern the ways they should enact this sort of missional love in their particular situations.

The second aspect of this spiritual practice of evangelism has to do with the nature of its liturgy—its worship. Of particular importance is the church's singing, since when we sing (as noted earlier), we pray twice. Let's take the old hymn of invitation, "Just as I Am," composed by Charlotte Elliott in 1835.[21] Three of the stanzas follow:

> Just as I am, without one plea,
> But that Thy blood was shed for me,
> And that Thou bidst me come to Thee,
> O Lamb of God, I come, I come.

> Just as I am, poor, wretched, blind;
> Sight, riches, healing of the mind,
> Yea, all I need in Thee to find,
> O Lamb of God, I come, I come.

> Just as I am, Thy love unknown
> Hath broken every barrier down;
> Now, to be Thine, yea, Thine alone,
> O Lamb of God, I come, I come.

These three stanzas affirm three aspects of the gospel of the crucified Messiah that implicitly challenge the gospel of "Make America Great Again" and other forms of civil religion. In stanza one, the invitation is to come to Jesus, the Lamb of God, not to any powerful "mighty eagle" (as in "Make America Great Again"). In the second stanza, the invitation is extended to, and received by, the weak—the poor, wretched, blind; they will be healed and fully satisfied, but there is no talk of pride and grandeur as the result. The last stanza attributes the breaking down of all barriers, not to national power or human effort, but to the love manifested on the cross. Ironically, this hymn has been a popular hymn of invitation in the Baptist tradition that also produced "Make America Great Again."

21. Elliot, "Just as I Am."

We can consider similarly a more recent piece of music commonly used in worship, "How Great Is Our God," by Chris Tomlin.[22] The mindset expressed in its lyrics is theologically robust and appropriate: it focuses on the triune God and God's greatness, not on a nation or people—or their past, present, or future greatness. Its symbolism is drawn from Revelation's depiction of Jesus as the lion of Judah and the slain lamb, not the American eagle. The song is an invitation to praise, a summons extended beyond national borders, to all the earth. Implicitly, the greatness spoken of here is—or should be—greatness as defined by the peculiar self-revelation of God in Jesus, in his cross and in his washing of feet.

Unfortunately, even a beautiful text can be mis-sung. "Our God" can be sung as "ours, not theirs." "Great" can be misunderstood in terms of political, economic, or military greatness. I have seen an eerie video of one hundred or more excited American soldiers singing this in a chapel service that was clearly meant to prepare them for something other than sharing the love of Jesus. Images of Jesus as the lion and the lamb can be misread as a view of Christ who slaughters enemies (lion) as well as one who died for sins (lamb), rather than as the One who expresses divine power in dying rather than killing. It is up to the Christian community and its leaders to prevent such mis-singing, which results in defective, dangerous formation and evangelism.

Conclusion

I have suggested in this chapter that cruciformity is a life-giving spiritual discipline that is the appropriate Christian alternative to civil religion. It is a form of abstinent engagement, of withdrawing from one thing to engage another. The discipline of cruciformity is focused both on the Christian community and its formation *and* on the world and its evangelization. May God grant the church, and each of us in it, the grace of missional, resurrectional cruciformity for the sake of the world—and our souls.

---

22. Tomlin, Reeves, and Cash, "How Great Is Our God."

Bibliography

Bonhoeffer, Dietrich. *The Cost of Discipleship*. New York: Simon and Schuster, 1995 (1959).

———. *Discipleship*. Dietrich Bonhoeffer Works 4. Translated by Barbara Green and Reinhard Krauss. Minneapolis: Augsburg Fortress, 2001.

Elliot, Charlotte. "Just as I Am." *Christian Remembrancer*, public domain, 1835.

Elliott, Neil, and Mark Reasoner, eds. *Documents and Images for the Study of Paul*. Minneapolis: Fortress, 2011.

Gardella, Peter. *American Civil Religion: What Americans Hold Sacred*. New York: Oxford University Press, 2014.

Gorman, Michael J. "Cruciformity." In *The Dictionary of Scripture and Ethics*, edited by Joel B. Green, 197–98. Grand Rapids: Baker Academic, 2011.

———. "Cruciformity according to Jesus and Paul." In *Unity and Diversity in the Gospels and Paul: Essays in Honor of Frank J. Matera*, edited by Christopher W. Skinner and Kelly R. Iverson, 173–201. SBLECL 7. Atlanta: Society of Biblical Literature, 2012.

———. *Cruciformity: Paul's Narrative Spirituality of the Cross*. 20th anniversary ed. Grand Rapids: Eerdmans, 2021 (2001).

———. *The Death of the Messiah and the Birth of the New Covenant: A (Not So) New Model of the Atonement*. Eugene, OR: Cascade, 2014.

———. *Participating in Christ: Explorations in Paul's Theology and Spirituality*. Grand Rapids: Baker Academic, 2019.

———. *Reading Revelation Responsibly: Uncivil Worship and Witness; Following the Lamb into the New Creation*. Eugene, OR: Cascade, 2011.

Laderman, Gary. *American Civil Religion*. Minneapolis: Fortress, 2012 (e-book).

Smith, James K. A. "The NFL's Thanksgiving Games Are a Spectacular Display of America's 'God and Country' Obsession." *Washington Post*, November 23, 2017. https://www.washingtonpost.com/news/acts-of-faith/wp/2017/11/23/the-nfls-thanksgiving-games-are-a-spectacular-display-of-americas-god-and-country-obsession/?noredirect=on&utm_term=.df5a7f7fe218.

Thomas, John Christopher. *Footwashing in John 13 and the Johannine Community*. 2nd ed. Cleveland, TN: Center for Pentecostal Theology, 2014.

Thomsen, Jacqueline. "Church Choir Sings 'Make America Great Again' Song to Trump." *The Hill*, July 2, 2017. https://thehill.com/blogs/blog-briefing-room/340451-choir-sings-make-america-great-again-song-to-trump/.

Tomlin, Chris, Jesse Reeves, and Ed Cash. "How Great Is Our God." Track 3 on *Arriving*. Sparrow, 2004.

Whitehead, Andrew L., and Samuel L. Perry. *Taking America Back for God: Christian Nationalism in the United States*. New York: Oxford University Press, 2020.

Willard, Dallas. *The Divine Conspiracy: Rediscovering Our Hidden Life in God*. New York: HarperCollins, 1998.

———. *The Spirit of the Disciplines: Understanding How God Changes Lives*. New York: HarperCollins, 1988.

Chapter 2

For the Good of the City

The Practice of Missional Discipleship

— Dave Witt

TrueCity, described in the introduction to this volume, has borne much fruit in Hamilton, Ontario. Since 2004, this network of churches has sought to strengthen congregations toward the goal of deeper engagement in various neighborhoods. Our missional vision is to let our hearts be broken by the things happening in our city that break God's heart. Broken hearts inspire action, and so we sing small songs into the splintered spaces we encounter. But we also want to operationalize missional theology, moving beyond academic discourse and putting it into practice. We seek to be "churches together for the good of the city" (following Jeremiah's command to "seek the welfare of the city"; Jer 29:7). I was part of the group that founded the network and have worked in the role of network developer since TrueCity began.

About ten years into the journey, we reflected on this ministry. To the good, we were encouraged to see our congregations more involved in initiatives such as welcoming refugees, tutoring in local schools, improving indigenous justice, increasing affordable housing, and decreasing food insecurity. We were learning a great deal about how commitment to prayer integrated with these initiatives, and how opportunities for evangelism flowed from them. And yet we were not seeing the kind of spiritual growth we knew was necessary to sustain this kind of engagement. Too many people were experiencing burnout as they dove into these new forms of mission. We were perhaps being influenced by the noisy, busy ways of the world. Many of us were expected to keep up other church roles alongside the new initiatives. Too often our missional engagement took the form of an individual cause, rather than being an integrated part of deeper spiritual community. We needed inspiration.

This was provided by Mike Breen. In his 2011 blog post "Why the Missional Movement Will Fail," he states that those of us looking to see churches join God in his mission had not counted the cost of what it would take to prepare our congregations to engage in this way.[1] If we really wanted to see everyone pursuing God's kingdom in our neighborhoods, we would have a greater need for discipleship. In Breen's estimation, most churches pursuing this kind of "missional" vision did not know how to integrate effective discipleship into the rhythms of mission-engaged church life.

Breen's challenge resonated with us and proved catalytic for the TrueCity network. In response, over a five-year period, a group of pastors and leaders from ten churches explored how to resource our churches for a new type of discipleship. One that had the range to connect with everyone interested and produce both deeper spiritual community and greater personal maturity. In this chapter I share the practices we experimented with as part of this TrueCity Missional Discipleship Project and what we learned in the process. I first look at the theology that underlies both mission and discipleship, and then describe three commitments that shaped our project.

Missional discipleship unfolds most fruitfully as communities respond to God's invitation to join him in his mission to reconcile all things to himself in Christ Jesus. I believe that the specific practices we commit to—immersing ourselves in Scripture, integrating prayer practices into daily life, and pursuing God's shalom intention for the world—will look different for different people. But all of us can develop natural rhythms of spiritual disciplines and missional practices as we seek to live our lives in and for Christ. Communal discipleship practices, if effective, lead to deeper relationships with Jesus and with each other, and deeper engagement with the world.

Input Shaping TrueCity's Missional Discipleship

Both the terms "missional" and "discipleship" are frequently misunderstood. The word "missional" has been used in so many ways that it is in danger of losing its usefulness. I believe that what makes it a fruitful

1. Breen, "Why the Missional Movement Will Fail."

concept is recognizing that God is on mission to reconcile all creation (Col 1:20), and that the church is formed by and for this mission. Similarly, while we might agree that discipleship is important, we are often vague about what is core to the practice. We need to understand that discipleship means committing to spiritual practices that give the Spirit freedom to move in our lives both individually and collectively, to develop Christlike character. We need to follow the model of Jesus, who intertwined mission and spirituality. As we abide in the vine, we will bear fruit.

Missional Theology

It is important to clarify the term "missional."[2] Foundational to our understanding is recognizing that sending is central to who God is. It is he who defines the nature of sending since God the Father sent the Son, and the Father and Son sent the Spirit.[3] The church is sent by the Spirit, as a kingdom ambassador, to join in God's mission.[4] This is captured by the term "*missio Dei*," meaning that God is on mission to bring creation to his full intention.[5] We need to pay attention to how Jesus lived out his mission and to follow his lead. Through the incarnation, not only is new life in Christ possible, but God in Christ shows us what kind of life he has empowered us to live. As Paul exhorts, we must have the same attitude as Christ (Phil 2:5). To summarize: "Mission simply means translating God's love in human form, putting every cultural tool—stories, symbols, attitudes, language, practices, and patterns of life—at the gospel's disposal."[6]

Such an understanding of mission involves a bigger framing of the Gospel, a recognition of the cosmic scope of what God has done in and through Christ. The Message captures this well: "All the broken and dislocated pieces—people and things, animals and atoms—get properly fixed and fit together in vibrant harmonies, all because of his death, his

---

2. Schoon helpfully highlights the connection of the Missional Church Movement to the Gospel and Our Culture Network and distinguishes this from five other streams that contribute to the broader understanding of the term "missional"; *Cultivating*, 19–39. See also Breen and Absalom, *Launching*, 21.

3. Editor's note: the theological debates around this concept are beyond the scope of this chapter.

4. Bosch, *Transforming*, 390.

5. Schoon, *Cultivating*, 19–20.

6. Dean, *Almost Christian*, 93, quoted in Maddix, "Missional Discipleship," 21.

blood that poured down from the cross" (Col 1:20, MSG). So, having an evangelistic conversation is not more or less an opportunity to participate in mission than advocating for the homeless, keeping the books for a corporation, or parenting a child.[7] There are many ways to "seek the welfare of our city" (Jer 29:7). The need is large and the songs we sing to fill it can be diverse and multiple sizes.

Missional theology rightly notes that the goal of mission is not primarily about extending and perpetuating the church. It is not a program of the church that the church controls. As Christopher Wright aptly observes, "Mission was not made for the church; the church was made for mission—God's mission."[8] This way of understanding mission demonstrates that any assumptions about the church as primarily an institution whose power we can use to shape culture are disappearing. The church is first and foremost God's people. We are at our best when living on the margins of culture, not necessarily as an institution, embracing opportunities to serve God and our neighbors.

Although missional theology promises a robust reframing of the identity and purpose of the church, insufficient work has been done to integrate these big ideas with practical daily living. Like other theology, it can too easily remain cerebral and never get grounded in practices. Old assumptions often continue to shape self-perception. When we view ourselves as the ones in control, "missional" gets mistakenly framed in terms of a new set of activities that a church commits to rather than as a shift in understanding who we are.[9]

This has certainly been a challenge for the churches involved in the TrueCity network. Especially in the early years of our work, we got caught up in the ways we could make a difference in our city by doing things like starting drop-in centers for poorer neighbors, running programs for local youth, and initiating outreach projects to connect with the urban Indigenous population. Such initiatives produced encouraging initial results but proved challenging to sustain over time. They were and continue to be good things to work at, but are dangerous if we use them to define who we are. It was too easy to pursue such activities as a badge of honor to prove ourselves rather than having them flow from a sense of God's leading. The difference is subtle, but significant. Missional discipleship is the necessary

---

7. Huckins and Yackley, *Thin Places*, 135.
8. Wright, *Mission of God*, 62.
9. Goheen, *Light to the Nations*, 4.

pathway for learning to distinguish between the two. We needed more and better resources to help us know how to practically work out such a significant paradigm shift. This is what makes engaging in missional discipleship so important.

Discipleship

Discipleship is the way that such missional insights move from intellectually held perspectives to lived reality. It describes the process of how disciples are made. I find the model of apprenticeship with its hands-on learning more helpful than the classroom education paradigm that we often use.[10] Churches have too rarely worked at defining this process and the practices required to form disciples. How do we equip individuals and groups to participate in the restorative and redemptive mission of God in the world?[11] We do well to interact with some of the insights arising from evangelicalism's emphasis on discipleship over the past seventy years.

This movement emphasizes equipping people with practices that over the centuries have proven effective in deepening one's spiritual life—prayer, Scripture study, witness, service, worship, discernment, and others. Richard Foster offers a paradigm for how we can engage them well: "God has given us the Disciplines of the spiritual life as a means of receiving his grace. The Disciplines allow us to place ourselves before God so that he can transform us."[12] It is not the disciplines themselves that renew us. Whichever disciplines we are led to practice, it is crucial that they act as a conduit for God's grace. We practice them to give the Spirit room to work in our lives.

This understanding of how the disciplines give God space is central to how we practice discipleship. And it is linked to the process of discipleship. As Dallas Willard reputedly said: "Since making disciples is the main task of every church, every church ought to be able to answer two questions. What is our plan for making disciples of Jesus? Is our plan working?" These two questions have encouraged missional church leaders to recognize the important role discipleship must play if congregations are to grow toward a more robust and integrated missional identity.[13]

10. Bowen, *Making Disciples Today*, 3–4.
11. Maddix, "Missional Discipleship," 18.
12. Foster, *Celebration of Discipline*, 25. Foster is a Quaker but his writing has been very influential in Western Evangelical Christianity.
13. Breen, "Why the Missional Movement Will Fail."

There are two primary weaknesses of past models that missional discipleship needs to address. First, classic discipleship models view the individual believer as the primary subject, and personal maturity as the goal. Community is valued as an outcome, but not considered crucial to the process itself. Truly vibrant, sustainable discipleship can only happen in the context of community. Healthy, committed relationships are both essential to the process and are a key indicator of maturity. Second, in classic discipleship models, mission is only viewed as an activity flowing from discipleship. It is not recognized as an important context within which discipleship happens. This understanding creates a false dichotomy that frequently pits mission and discipleship against each other. Often, key discipleship practices do not adequately address how we are called to join with God in his mission. Consequently, mission is understood as an add-on. What we need is to draw on the best of these discipleship models, but with additional practices that move us toward the goal of seeing communities of disciples discerning how they are called to join with God in his mission both individually and together. This leads us to the spiritual practice of missional discipleship.

Fruitful Missional Discipleship Practice

Ten years into collaborating on missional experiments, our TrueCity network saw a growing number of people creatively engaged in pursuing the good of our city. There was the group from five different churches that started Micah House in order to provide shelter and support for refugees when they first arrived in our city, the artists from a number of churches that got involved with various studios involved in a monthly art crawl, the food security group that ran weekly community meals as part of their neighborhood drop-in times, and the churches that partnered with a local agency to create affordable housing. These are all great initiatives that continue to bear good fruit, but we found that running them was taking a toll on those most involved. We understood the importance of the missional critique, and the shift in church practices it called for, but did not yet have an adequate process of discipleship that was consistent with these shifts.

Therefore, we initiated the TrueCity Discipleship Project in order to find congregationally based discipleship practices that led people into missional lifestyles and equipped them to grow. This project provided pastors with a model of discipleship that integrated spiritual formation, community building, and missional engagement. From 2015 to 2019 a cohort of five to seven pastors and church leaders participated in a yearlong "huddle" process, meeting weekly to study, reflect, and engage mission together.[14] These huddle groups continued to meet for another year of coaching and support as participants started discipleship groups in their own churches. Many of those who participated in this two-year process have continued to meet in peer mentoring groups. One of the pastors who was involved reflected: "Joining in the huddle process gave me the tools I was looking for to help make missional discipleship a more accessible reality in our congregation, but more than that, the experience with other pastors took me deeper in my walk with Jesus."

There are three principles that we found helpful:

- practicing discipleship in communities that are committed to pursue mission together
- centering discipleship around communal discernment; identifying how the Spirit is speaking and how we can best respond as we live out our shared sense of mission
- doing discipleship in multi-church cohorts that strengthens our commitment to being a network of churches engaged in missional collaboration

I believe that any church aspiring to respond to God's invitation to join him in his mission will want to practice discipleship that integrates these three practices. We examine these in turn.

Forming and Centering Life in Communities

As mentioned, evangelical discipleship movements tend to frame spiritual formation individualistically. However, robust missional discipleship is primarily corporate and secondarily individual. As Lesslie Newbigin observes, Jesus did not write a book with rules for us to follow but formed a community that is the hermeneutic of the Gospel.[15] Good missional discipleship recognizes the body of Christ as both the primary location of

---

14. We used 3DM materials and methodology. This decentralized movement, founded by Mike Breen, aims to equip churches for missional engagement through discipleship and church development. Breen's book, *Building a Discipleship Culture*, has been a core resource for the TrueCity Discipleship Project.

15. Newbigin, *Gospel*, 227.

spiritual formation and a measure of the outcomes of the process. Breen and Absalom describe this well: "We are designed to not only live in community but also to be at our most fruitful there. It should come as no great surprise to discover that we will usually be most effective missionally when we go with others. Put simply, we go as a community, inviting people into community."[16] Furthermore, our identities are shaped by the communities that we identify with. As Christopher Beard states, "The reality of identity formation, and therefore spiritual formation, is that the communities we participate in play a paramount role in that formation, regardless of the identity of the community. . . . Missional discipleship, therefore, must include learning in community."[17]

David Fitch describes such communities from a different angle. He highlights how Christians need to let go of the power-grabbing posture that has become our reputation and instead enter into dialogue in a way that makes us a faithful presence. He argues convincingly that such presence must be communal to be sustainable.[18] Fitch describes three spaces we are called to inhabit as communities:

- A "close circle" where Christians discern their submission to Christ and each other; our social closeness is not intended to be closed to outsiders but will primarily be inhabited by the community of faith. We experienced this in our huddle groups as part of the TrueCity discipleship project, and then replicated these huddles in our various congregations.

- A "dotted circle" where committed followers make space for neighbors and strangers to enter in and observe how God is at work in the community. Our goal was to launch "missional communities" that have an ongoing mission-centered presence. Through church endeavors, such as sponsoring and supporting refugee families, we created easily accessible points for neighbors and other acquaintances to join in.

- A "half circle" where Christians go among the world as guests. "Here we discern Christ's presence as a guest among the hurting and the wandering. In this half circle the question is never whether Christ

---

16. Breen and Absalom, *Launching*, 29.
17. Beard, "Missional Discipleship," 184.
18. Fitch, *Faithful Presence*, 12–14.

is here or not. Rather it is whether his presence will be welcomed."[19] In Hamilton, these are places like neighborhood associations, school councils, and various advocacy groups. Places where we see Christ already present and at work, where our neighbors are already pursuing the good of our city, and where we can respond to their invitation to join in.

Fitch's work reinforces the contention that missional discipleship will be most effective when done in the context of community.

One encouraging example from our Discipleship Project was the missional community that worked with its neighbors to apply for a park beautification grant. However, we are still early in the process of seeing missional discipleship thoroughly integrated into the core structuring of our churches. Our yearlong experience in discipleship huddles has proven readily transferable, but starting and sustaining missional communities that engage both discipleship and mission on an ongoing basis are still a work in progress. It is a long, slow endeavor that is best done collaboratively. The hyper-individualism that characterizes our culture creates both a pervasive longing for community and a resistance to committing and submitting to it—in short, a splintering. Our experience of cohort learning in the TrueCity Discipleship Project supports my belief that missional discipleship is best done communally. As challenging as it is to create and sustain such communities, prioritizing this practice is crucial if we hope to see missional discipleship fruitfully integrated into church life.

Collective Discernment

The second practice that we found bore good fruit as part of the Discipleship Project was a commitment to collective discernment. This is one of Foster's corporate spiritual disciplines that he names guidance and describes as listening to the Holy Spirit.[20] We intentionally shared situations during our weeks in which we felt that God wanted our attention. We would then discern how the Spirit was using those experiences to give us direction.

One specific activity is to identify "*kairos* moments." This discipleship tool, based on the Greek word that describes a specific time of grace and

---

19. Fitch, *Faithful Presence*, 40–41.
20. Foster, *Celebration*, 175–89.

opportunity, embeds reflexive praxis in the discipleship process.[21] It challenges us to be alert for "non-neutral" moments in the midst of our days and to ask ourselves, "What is Jesus saying to me?" This is a two-stage process. It starts with a turning/repentance movement, which involves awareness, reflection, and discussion, and continues with a believing/action movement that takes us through the steps of planning, accounting, and acting.[22] We used this reflexive praxis model consistently over the five years of the project and it proved extremely fruitful in integrating missional discipleship into our daily lives. For example, one pastor felt overwhelming grief while interacting with some of his son's high school friends. Praying into those emotions led him to conduct research that revealed a lack of churches where second-generation immigrant youth could encounter the Gospel. Another church leader shared his frustration with his church's leadership processes. As he prayed, he realized that the time commitments his leadership role demanded were creating fear about shortchanging his family.

Most *kairos* moments are not as large as these. Often they are blips of emotion amidst the minutia of life that God uses to get our attention, challenging us to change.[23] Thus we become aware of our part in the narrative of God's work in the world. This world in which the incarnation, life, death, and resurrection of Jesus Christ are the culmination and center. Collective discernment equips us to recognize and celebrate this melody to which all our lives are to harmonize.[24] It moves the pursuit of participation in the *missio Dei* from a cerebral consideration into our daily lived reality. It gives us the opportunity and responsibility to reflect on how and where we are joining God in his mission.

Collective discernment engages people in the midst of life. It is not about information download, but is something that is experienced. We synthesize information and practice in a way that reinforces and deepens our learning experience. This nonlinear process adapts well to the ebb and flow of life and is particularly effective for adult learning.[25] For this reason, it is a practice ideally suited to missional discipleship.

Communal discernment enables us to better recognize that our part in God's mission is not distinguished by our types of activity, but by our

---

21. Breen, *Building*, 76.
22. Breen, *Building*, 80–84.
23. Beard, "Missional Discipleship," 178.
24. Hirsh and Hirsh, *Untamed*, 28.
25. Beard, "Missional Discipleship," 181–83.

submission to God's presence and leading. It helps us overcome the church's past tendency to understand mission as a separate activity or type of programming. Fitch's three circles, described above, illustrate the different postures we need to discern in practicing core disciplines. By engaging in this reflection/action discernment process during formal and informal times together, we can better understand the nature of the part we are invited to play in the *missio Dei* individually and collectively. This practice prioritizes the question of what our partnership with God calls forth in the particulars of our lives.[26] Integrating collective discernment into missional discipleship enables us to participate better in God's work. It helps us develop healthier rhythms of spiritual discipline and mission.

Multi-Church Cohort Learning

The final fruitful practice that the Discipleship Project revealed is the importance of enriching interdependence between churches through multi-church cohort learning. By prioritizing practices that emphasize cooperation between churches, rather than competition, we can better recognize the multifaceted nature of God's work in our cities.

Many churches had expressed a longing for more robust congregational expressions of missional discipleship. In response, the TrueCity Discipleship Project formed multi-congregational cohorts. This was initially a more pragmatic consideration than an intentional attempt to unify the network. But by the third year we realized that the process was strengthening key relationships between pastors of congregations with significant differences. So, while there was not specific content that focused on enriching the interdependence of churches, by working within a network and including multiple congregations, the process accomplished this. Cohort learning and ongoing peer mentoring allowed us to learn from a range of creative initiatives and to compare notes when encountering challenges. No two churches are the same, so having multiple examples of how to implement missional discipleship is essential. The honesty and depth of sharing that we experienced in the first year's discipleship process created a context of ongoing encouragement. Praying with and for each other regularly has been life-giving.

If we believe that the unity of the church is important to God and is a powerful witness in our context, we need to have discipleship practices

26. Beard, "Missional Discipleship," 180.

that lead to deeper relationships with other churches. One practice is to make theological dialogue part of our ongoing discipleship work. Interfaith consultant Richard Sudworth testifies that when we bring both a strong commitment to our own tradition and an openness to others into dialogue with those who hold to traditions different than ours, we build bridges and deepen our understandings of our own traditions. "It is not about denying differences nor eliminating distinctives, but about encountering the Other in a mutually learning, yet challenging atmosphere."[27] Listening is the key practice in this pursuit.[28] It involves attending simultaneously to the person we are interacting with, our own tradition, and the Holy Spirit. This is something our Discipleship Project aims to explore further.

Our churches have been enriched by the relationships we have formed across our differences. We have seen collaboration flow from these groups. On one occasion, three churches held a joint Christmas Eve service; on another, one church lent a huddle leader to another to facilitate that church's discipleship project. Through functioning as a network, the churches involved in TrueCity have realized that each congregation has different gifts and strengths as well as needs and blind spots. This is the beauty of differentiated unity. It both enriches congregations through their interaction with each other, and in the process strengthens the body of Christ.[29] Collaboratively working at missional discipleship, as with our Discipleship Project, has shown us that the more we recognize our unity as a given reality and our differences as potentially enriching, the more fruitful our collective efforts can be.

Conclusion

My experience working with TrueCity continues to be both challenging and rewarding. Through the Discipleship Project and its communal practices, my faith has deepened and my relationships with other leaders has been enriched. It has provided concrete opportunities to live out my conviction that mission and discipleship are intertwined. They are most fruitfully practiced in the context of communities that practicing multi-church

---

27. Sudworth, "Missional Discipleship," 88.

28. Huckins and Yackley recommend listening as the first of six postures essential for missional formation; the others are submerging, inviting, contending, imagining, and entrusting; *Thin Places*.

29. Van Gelder, *Essence*, 122.

learning, missional collaboration, and collective discernment. These spiritual practices help us understand how we can respond to the Spirit's leading as we live out our shared sense of mission. As we grow spiritually, we better understand God's song, and our voices are strengthened to sing this song to the world. It is through these daily and weekly rhythms of individual and communal spiritual practices that we can participate ever more fully in God's mission to reconcile all creation to himself in Christ. This involves committing to a set of practices in order to open our lives to God's gracious, transforming initiative. Such discipleship is essential for taking the big picture aspiration of participation in the *missio Dei* and grounding it in the lived reality of congregational life. I am excited to have the opportunity to continue to be engaged with a network of churches that are pursuing this reality together and, in this way, give the Spirit freedom to move powerfully among us for the good of our city.

Bibliography

Beard, Christopher. "Missional Discipleship: Discerning Spiritual-Formation Practices and Goals Within the Missional Movement." *Missiology: An International Review* 43 (2015) 175–94.

Bosch, David. *Transforming Mission: Paradigm Shifts in Theology of Mission*. Maryknoll, NY: Orbis, 1997.

Bowen, John. *Making Disciples Today: What, Why and How . . . on Earth?* North York: Wycliffe Booklets, 2013.

Breen, Mike. *Building a Discipleship Culture*. 3rd ed. Pawleys Island, SC: 3DM, 2017.

———. "Why the Missional Movement Will Fail." Vergenetwork (blog), September 14, 2011. http://www.vergenetwork.org/2011/09/14/mike-breen-why-the-missional-movement-will-fail/.

Breen, Mike, and Alex Absalom. *Launching Missional Communities: A Field Guide*. Pawleys Island, SC: 3DM, 2010.

Fitch, David E. *Faithful Presence: Seven Disciplines that Shape the Church for Mission*. Downers Grove, IL: InterVarsity, 2016.

Foster, Richard J. *Celebration of Discipline: The Path to Spiritual Growth*. Special Anniversary Edition. San Francisco: HarperOne, 2018.

Goheen, Michael. *A Light to the Nations: The Missional Church and the Biblical Story*. Grand Rapids: Baker Academic, 2011.

Hirsch, Alan, and Debra Hirsch. *Untamed: Reactivating a Missional Form of Discipleship*. Grand Rapids: Baker, 2010.

Huckins, Jon, and Rob Yackley. *Thin Places: Six Postures for Creating and Practicing Missional Community*. Kansas City, MO: House Studio, 2012.

Maddix, Mark A. "Missional Discipleship." In *Missional Discipleship* edited by Mark A. Maddix and Jay Richard Akkerman, 15–26. Kansas City: Beacon, 2013.

Newbigin, Leslie. *The Gospel in a Pluralist Society*. Grand Rapids: Eerdmans, 1989.

Schoon, Christopher James. *Cultivating an Evangelistic Character: Integrating Worship and Discipleship in the Missional Movement.* Eugene, OR: Wipf & Stock, 2018.

Sudworth, Richard J. "Missional Discipleship: Following Christ the Lord in a Multi-faith Society." *Anvil* 25 (2008) 85–94.

Van Gelder, Craig. *The Essence of the Church: A Community Created by the Spirit.* Grand Rapids: Baker, 2000.

Wright, Christopher J. H. *The Mission of God: Unlocking the Bible's Grand Narrative.* Downers Grove, IL: IVP Academic, 2006.

Chapter 3

Joining Jesus

Prayer as Mission and the Mission of Prayer

MICHAEL P. KNOWLES

AS OFTEN AS NOT, discussion of prayer begins with practical considerations, in particular the question of *how* we ought to pray—what to ask for and what words we should use. There is certainly good precedent for this approach: "One of his disciples said to him, 'Lord, teach us to pray, as John taught his disciples'" (Luke 11:1). But when it comes to prayer, theology is at least as important as method—only when we have a clear sense of *why* we pray, and of what prayer hopes to accomplish, will we gain a clearer sense of *how* to pray, and what to pray for. From a theological perspective, the purpose of prayer becomes clearer in relation to mission (the mission of God in particular), so situating prayer in that context helps us not only to understand prayer better, but also to practice it more faithfully. To put this another way: prayer is the means by which we seek to ensure that the church's mission, by which we respond to the needs of a suffering world, is fully in line with Christ's own response to a suffering and splintered world. The age-old conflict between action and contemplation, mission or prayer, disappears when we recognize that adoration and activism alike are both initiated and sustained by God. If Christian mission must be rooted in prayer, prayer itself must be rooted in the mission of God.

Prayer and the Way of the World

When Jesus teaches his disciples to pray, "May *your* kingdom come, may *your* will be done" (Matt 6:10), the obvious inference is that someone other than God has taken charge and someone else's will is being done, whether that of the Roman military in Jesus's day, secular forces today, or a rebellious humanity in general. In Jewish and Christian theology, "heaven and the heaven of heavens belong to the Lord," as does "the earth with all that is in it."[1] Psalm 115:16, on the other hand, offers a more nuanced account: "The heavens are the Lord's heavens, but the earth he has given to human beings." Or as Psalm 8:5–6 explains, "You have made them a little lower than God . . . you have given them dominion over the works of your hands." In other words, God has given the whole of creation into our care—so completely so that God's presence is not obvious and people are free to conduct their lives as though God did not exist. We can think of our situation in terms of the parable Jesus tells about tenant farmers who take over the vineyard in which they work:

> A man planted a vineyard, put a fence around it, dug a pit for the wine press, and built a watchtower; then he leased it to tenants and went to another country. When the season came, he sent a slave to the tenants to collect from them his share of the produce of the vineyard. But they seized him, and beat him, and sent him away empty-handed. And again he sent another slave to them; this one they beat over the head and insulted. Then he sent another, and that one they killed. And so it was with many others; some they beat, and others they killed. He had still one other, a beloved son. Finally he sent him to them, saying, "They will respect my son." But those tenants said to one another, "This is the heir; come, let us kill him, and the inheritance will be ours." So they seized him, killed him, and threw him out of the vineyard. (Mark 12:1–8)

In similar fashion, God invites the first humans to "Be fruitful and multiply, and fill the earth and subdue it; and have dominion over the fish of the sea and over the birds of the air and over every living thing that moves upon the earth" (Gen 1:28). But rather than exercising responsible stewardship and acknowledging their obligations and responsibilities toward the Creator and true Lord of the earth, the servants take charge of creation as though it were their own, to do with as they please. They divide various territories among themselves and spend the rest of their time bickering over who should be

---

1. E.g., Deut 10:14; cf. Ps 24:1; 50:12; 89:11; 1 Cor 10:26.

in charge of what. We are like the household steward who helps himself to provisions and does violence to his fellow slaves when the master's return is temporarily delayed (Matt 24:48–51). Yet as with the owner of the vineyard in the parable, all that God asks of us is an acknowledgement that we owe our well-being to the true Lord of heaven and earth.

Framing the situation in this manner yields our first important insight into the practical dimensions of missional prayer. Prayer always proceeds from the perspective of a broken and rebellious creation; it begins with our acknowledgement, in the wonderful language of Miles Coverdale's 1535 translation, that "all the foundations of the earth are out of course" (Ps 82:5).[2] Returning to the imagery of Jesus's parable, we confess that we have arrogated ownership of the vineyard to ourselves, corrupted the land, misappropriated its produce, and abused our fellow servants, acting as though the true Master were not planning to return any time soon. We acknowledge that our claims of ownership are wholly false, give back what we have seized to its rightful owner, and plead for God to restore the justice and harmony that obtain only under his tutelage and sovereignty.

In this sense, prayer is always an expression of penitence. We pray, as often as not, because things are out of control: the cancer has returned, the relationship is irreconcilable, the violent have triumphed, someone we love has died. Pain, or sorrow, or shame, or simple weakness overwhelm us. We long for order and justice. The answer is not always the one we look for: neither justice nor healing come easily, and some aspects of salvation will not precede our own death or the Lord's return (whichever comes first). But to pray in the presence and on behalf of a broken creation is to yield ourselves in hope to God's promised future for a restored and reconciled humanity. Instead of trying to fix things ourselves (since our attempt to commandeer creation is what created such problems in the first place), we confess that our only hope of restoration lies in submitting instead to God: "May *your* kingdom come; may *your* will be done."

So rather than seizing control unilaterally (on the one hand) or abandoning control altogether (on the other), taking our rightful place before God in prayer is a matter of exercising the authority that has in fact been granted us, but doing so in the appropriate manner by submitting our own, delegated authority to the greater authority of God. If we have wrongly taken control of our world (theologically speaking), we alone are in a position to yield it back, acknowledging that everything we

---

2. Quoted (here and subsequently) from *Book of Common Prayer*, in loc.

possess—including life itself—is a gift from God. Our model for doing so is Jesus himself, at prayer in the garden of Gethsemane, as three times he cries out to his Father, "Not my will but yours be done" (Luke 22:42; cf. Matt 26:39-44; Mark 14:35-41). At Gethsemane, Jesus leads us in the struggle to submit to the reign of God, yielding to the will of the Father even when he knows that doing so will cost him his life.

In practical terms, this explains why breakthroughs in the spiritual life so often come at moments of crisis and need. In moments such as these, we experience the dreadful consequences of human domination (our own, that of others, and all humanity with us) in place of God's gracious dominion. At moments of personal and societal urgency, the illusion of human control is revealed for what it is—an illusion on the part of some, an abomination on the part of others, but in any case a power struggle in which some insist on winning at the expense of those who must lose. So we turn to the One to whom true dominion belongs, yielding at last to the One who has yielded to us: "Turn us again, O Lord God of hosts; show the light of thy countenance, and we shall be whole" (Ps 80:19, Coverdale). This is the situation as we bow in prayer, apart from which our prayer would not have been necessary in the first place.

Prayer and the Will of God

On the face of it, prayer looks for all the world like a human attempt to change the mind or will of God: "Lord, bless this mess." Yet whether or not this is so, prayer first entails a change of *human* minds and wills: "Lord, have it your way; not our will but yours be done." If we are not careful, we will be tempted to think of the God to whom we pray as a somewhat hard-hearted old man who must be wheedled, cajoled, or otherwise compelled into doing what he otherwise might not. According to this view of things, our reassurance consists in the fact that God finds the name of Jesus irresistible: it is the key to the gates of heaven, and so we must employ it at every turn (at least once at the start or finish of every sentence in our prayer).

But wielding the name of Jesus in this way overlooks what the name itself intends. As is often the case, the apostle Paul says it best: "While we were still sinners, Christ died for us" (Rom 5:8). In other words, long before the possibility of prayer occurred to us (or we ourselves occurred to our parents), God had already taken the initiative to provide an answer that is "far more than all we can ask or imagine" (Eph 3:20). This is why Paul can tell the believers at ancient Corinth that in Christ, "every one of God's promises is a 'Yes'" (2 Cor 1:19). In other words, Jesus himself is the proof of God's willingness to rescue humanity from the mess we have made.

Understanding that Jesus is already God's answer changes our view of prayer. Our instinct is to assume that once we put our request into words, God must decide how to respond. A more pious explanation would be that God always answers our requests, but not necessarily the way we want. This view is captured nicely in a familiar aphorism from Book One of the spiritual classic, *The Imitation of Christ*: "Man proposes but God disposes."[3] The critical assumption here is that prayer is primarily a matter of human initiative that awaits a divine response.

Yet Christian theologians have always insisted that, at a deeper level, it is God who initiates prayer: prayer really begins with God searching for a lost humanity and preemptively reconciling creation to himself. Had God not already made himself known, above all in Jesus, we would likely not bother and certainly not know how to pray. Seeing matters this way makes a considerable difference to the prayers themselves. If prayer is something we initiate, we have no way of knowing how God will respond. Even if we feel sure that God will be favorably disposed to our prayer (because we have the right attitude or sufficient faith, or because we employ appropriate language and appeal to the name of his Son), there is still no certainty as to whether God will pay attention on this particular occasion, in response to this particular plea.

But what if we know that God has already made the first move? Far from needing to be roused from slumber (1 Kgs 18:27) or turned aside from more pressing business elsewhere, God is the one who has been waiting for us all along, not the other way around. In the familiar parable of the prodigal son (Luke 15:11–32), Jesus offers a compelling illustration of God's desire for reconciliation and restoration. The social and religious customs of Jesus's day required that a returning sinner offer proof of sufficient remorse or penitence. Accordingly, the father in the parable should have remained at home with his older, more obedient son. Now disowned and disgraced, the younger son must plead for readmission to his father's house, with no one to blame but himself. This is exactly what the prodigal himself expects, as he carefully rehearses his speech each step of the way back from the "far country." But against all expectation, the father spies his returning son while he is still in the distance—the old man must have stood

---

3. à Kempis, *Imitation of Christ*, 20.

waiting, every day, at the city gate—and instead of maintaining his dignity, dishonors himself by running headlong down the road, throwing his arms around his son, and showering him with kisses. He even cuts off his son's speech with a command that the celebrations begin.

We may gauge how radical the father's behavior is from the outrage of the elder brother. As he sees it, his father should not have welcomed him back at all, or at least not until the wayward son had given him ample reason for doing so. In keeping with our intuitive sense of how prayer and petition normally work, the father should not have listened to a word until the younger brother had proven that he deserved to be heard. Full restitution of all losses to the family estate would have been a good start. This is our natural instinct when we come before a holy God, the one whom Jesus taught us to address as "our Father." We fear that we haven't changed enough, that we aren't sorry or sincere enough, and that we cannot muster sufficient reasons for God to bother with us. But the point of the parable—at least as it applies to prayer—is that our hope of being graciously heard lies not in us or in anything we bring, but rather in the character and heart of an impossibly gracious God. Like the prodigal's shameless father, the Father of Jesus stands waiting, longing for our return.

The consistent testimony of Scripture is that God is already "merciful and gracious, slow to anger, and abounding in steadfast love and faithfulness . . . forgiving iniquity and transgression and sin" before (as well as after) we pray (so Exod 34:6–7 and many other passages that echo its language). This is what Israel discovers in the course of its long and checkered history; this is what Jesus means when he says, "Whoever has seen me has seen the Father" (John 14:9); and it is on this basis that God invites us to bring our many needs to him. As Richard Foster observes, far from trying to force concessions from an unwilling deity, "Prayer is the human *response* to the perpetual outpouring of love by which God lays siege to every soul."[4]

Prayer and the Ministry of Jesus

Jesus, the incarnate Son of God, quite literally embodies God's desire to reconcile humanity to himself (2 Cor 5:19). By virtue of his incarnation, Jesus is not simply a personal emissary from the Father: he is the very *missio Dei* ("mission of God") in human form. For this reason, Jesus's own mission of divine-human reconciliation is expressed not just in the fact

---

4. Foster, *Prayer*, 81 (emphasis original).

that he takes on human form, not only in his cross and resurrection, but also (as an extension of his earthly ministry) by his unceasing prayer and intercession on behalf of humanity. The letter to the Hebrews explains, "In the days of his flesh, Jesus offered up prayers and supplications, with loud cries and tears, to the one who was able to save him from death, and he was heard because of his reverent submission" (Heb 5:7). Becoming human, with all its frailties and uncertainties, required prayer as much for Jesus as for the rest of us. But the writer then goes on to say that because his status as a perfect high priest is unchanging, and because his own life offers a perfect sacrifice for sin, "he is able for all time to save those who approach God through him, since he always lives to make intercession for them" (Heb 7:25). Just as prayer was essential to his human existence, so Jesus continues to pray as he takes his place in the throne room of God. In his commentary on this passage, Anglican bishop and New Testament scholar Brooke Foss Westcott (1825–1901) comments, "He pleads our cause with the Father . . . and makes the prayers heard which we know not how to shape."[5] Using the same language as the letter to the Hebrews, Paul explains Jesus's ongoing prayer as the consequence of his sacrificial death and resurrection: "Who will bring any charge against God's elect? It is God who justifies. Who is to condemn? It is Christ Jesus, who died, yes, who was raised, who is at the right hand of God, who indeed intercedes for us" (Rom 8:33–34). Just as in Hebrews, Jesus's sacrifice for sin and his ongoing intercession are directly linked: even as he has fulfilled the will of the Father "once for all" (So Rom 6:10; Heb 7:27; 9:12; 10:10), he continues to put that saving work into effect on a case-by-case basis. In both his earthly life and his heavenly intercession, Jesus thus demonstrates the perfect balance between contemplation and action: prayer undergirds his ministry of healing and reconciliation; his reconciliation of heaven and earth provides the basis for his ongoing prayer before the Father. In the words of Karl Barth, "All our prayers are summed up in Jesus Christ: God cannot fail to answer because it is Christ who prays."[6]

But if Jesus has already reconciled us to God and continues to intercede on our behalf, what room is left for the prayers of the saints? Since we will never be able to out-pray the beloved Son of God, all that remains is for us to join our prayers with those that Jesus continually offers on our behalf. We allow our prayers to be shaped by his, and when our own

---

5. Westcott, *Epistle to the Hebrews*, 192.
6. Barth, *Prayer and Preaching*, 18.

words fail, we ask him to articulate what we ourselves cannot. In fact (allowing for a degree of Trinitarian overlap), this is how Paul explains the work of the Spirit in facilitating prayer: "Likewise the Spirit helps us in our weakness; for we do not know how to pray as we ought, but that very Spirit intercedes with sighs too deep for words. And God, who searches the heart, knows what is the mind of the Spirit, because the Spirit intercedes for the saints according to the will of God" (Rom 8:26–27). Again, prayer is less a matter of trying to sway God's will in answer to our needs than one of joining our prayers to those of the Son and Spirit, discovering as we do so that divine mercy has not only anticipated our concerns, but has already fully provided for them. It is on this basis that Paul can exhort us to "pray without ceasing" (1 Thess 5:17): since Jesus himself prays without ceasing, part of the long and slow process of our becoming like the Son in all things is learning to pray likewise, as beloved children of our heavenly Father. To pray this way is to understand not only that our ministries must be undergirded with prayer, but that prayer and ministry alike are sustained by the ongoing work of Christ.

Simply put, the mission of Jesus is to return a wayward creation—with its fragile and rebellious creatures—to their holy and gracious creator. Whether we think of this in forensic terms, as forgiveness and reconciliation; in organic and existential terms as a matter of new birth, new creation, and new identity; or in dynamic terms as being reoriented to the ways of God and joining in God's active mission to heal the world and redress its injustices, our basic disposition as disciples and "followers" of Jesus is that we allow him to take the lead in all things. Prayer is no exception. From this perspective, the prayers that we offer for a broken world are less an expression of our own or the church's mission, undertaken on behalf of Christ, than they are a means by which we join Jesus as he ministers in obedience to and on behalf of the Father. In other words, we do not pray *in order* to render God merciful toward us and our neighbors; quite the opposite, we pray *because* Christ has already demonstrated God's mercy and has been interceding for us all along. In essence, prayer is not the *cause* of grace, but its *consequence*.

The greatest surprise in prayer is not simply that God is kind enough to answer us, but that our vision both of ourselves and of God is transformed as we pray. Even though we may initially be preoccupied with whatever need or concern or failure inspires prayer in the first place, drawing near to Jesus as Jesus draws us near to the Father reassures us of God's bountiful compassion, kindness, and abundant provision for human need. Just so, the English mystic Julian of Norwich (1342–ca. 1416) marvels that God answers prayer not grudgingly or under protest, but out of delight and rejoicing that Christ has already provided for every possible need. She imagines Jesus inviting us to share in his own and the Father's delight that his ministry provides the assurance of answered prayer:

> My darling, look and see your Lord, your God, who is your maker and your endless joy. . . . See what delight and bliss I have in your salvation. . . . Now all my bitter pain and all my hard labour is turned into endless joy and bliss for me and for you. How could it now be that you could pray to me for anything that pleased me which I would not gladly grant you?[7]

Prayer That Longs with God: Listening, Speaking, and Waiting

One of the very few Aramaic words that survive in the New Testament (although transliterated into Greek) is "Abba"—"Father"—which we find both on the lips of Jesus in the garden of Gethsemane (Mark 14:36) and in Paul's letters as the simplest of all prayers, one that expresses our essential identity as children of a heavenly Father:

> You did not receive a spirit of slavery to fall back into fear, but you have received a spirit of adoption. When we cry, "Abba! Father!" it is that very Spirit bearing witness with our spirit that we are children of God, and if children, then heirs, heirs of God and joint heirs with Christ—if, in fact, we suffer with him so that we may also be glorified with him. (Rom 8:14–17; cf. Gal 4:4–6)

In effect, Paul is explaining what Jesus meant when he taught his disciples to begin their own prayers by calling God "Father" (Matt 6:9; Luke 11:2). Since children are not, by definition, self-made, praying in this manner amounts to an acknowledgement of our spiritual paternity, as we confess that our very existence is a consequence and overflow of the Father's rich love.

Our *identity* as children of God and our *ministry* as those who pray to the Father thus operate on the same basis: who we are and how we speak are both consequences of what Christ has done for us, rather than expressions of what we choose to accomplish for the sake of Christ. This

---

7. Julian of Norwich, *Revelations of Divine Love*, §24, 72.

unexpectedly simple (if radical) principle yields our next major insight into the conduct of prayer. Before it involves speaking, prayer first requires that we listen (and the silence that listening requires is a spiritual discipline of its own). Rather than taking the initiative—"storming heaven," as is sometimes proposed—prayer that is attuned to the mission of God waits quietly, attentive to the impetus of the Spirit, in order to know what to say. A prayer of the Russian Orthodox Metropolitan Philaret of Moscow (1782–1867) models this approach:

> O Lord, I know not what to ask of thee. Thou alone knowest what are my true needs. Thou lovest me more than I myself know how to love. Help me to see my real needs which are concealed from me. I dare not ask either a cross or a consolation. I can only wait on thee. My heart is open to thee. Visit and help me, for thy great mercy's sake. Strike me and heal me, cast me down and raise me up. I worship in silence thy holy will and thine inscrutable ways. I offer myself as a sacrifice to thee. I put all my trust in thee. I have no other desire than to fulfill thy will. Teach me how to pray. Pray thou thyself in me.[8]

In fact, this is how Jesus conducts his own ministry, as he explains to his disciples in the Gospel of John: "The Son can do nothing on his own, but only what he sees the Father doing; whatever the Father does, the Son does likewise" (John 5:19).[9] Jesus consistently confesses his complete inability apart from the Father: his mission and ministry consist of beholding, copying, and participating in the saving purpose of the Father. The same, he says, must be true between himself and his followers, especially when it comes to prayer:

> Just as the branch cannot bear fruit by itself unless it abides in the vine, neither can you unless you abide in me. I am the vine, you are the branches. Those who abide in me and I in them bear much fruit, because apart from me you can do nothing.... If you abide in me, and my words abide in you, *ask for whatever you wish*, and it will be done for you. (John 4–5, 7; emphasis added)

Even prayer, says Jesus, is less a matter of striving or pleading than of resting, waiting, and trusting in union with him. In a sense, therefore, neither prayer nor the faith that prayer requires are ultimately dependent on us.

---

8. *Manual of Eastern Orthodox Prayers*, 24.

9. Cf. John 5:30 ("I can do nothing on my own"); 8:28 ("I do nothing on my own, but I speak ... as the Father instructed me").

Julian of Norwich realizes as much when she wrestles with the weakness and uncertainty of her own prayers: "Our Lord brought all this suddenly to mind and revealed these words and said, 'I am the foundation of your prayers: first, it is my will that you should have something, and then I make you desire it, and then I make you pray for it. And if you pray for it, how then could it be that you should not have what you pray for?'"[10] As the life of Jesus flows into us, refreshing us and refashioning us into his image, we thus begin to understand his purpose; moved by his love, we begin to yearn over a creation estranged from its Creator. Then, in unison with Jesus, we pray for God to exert his reign and accomplish his will here on earth. In the words of the nineteenth-century missionary to North Africa, Lilias Trotter (1853–1928), "If we can listen in the stillness, till our hearts begin to vibrate to what he is feeling about the matter in question, whether it concerns ourselves or others, we can, from that moment, begin to pray down from his throne."[11]

To join our prayers with those of Jesus means entering into the suffering and sorrow of God, longing *with* God for redemption, being made part of the salvation established in Jesus through his own submission to the injustice and evil of the world. To pray, therefore, is not to "heap up empty phrases as the Gentiles do" (Matt 6:7), but to be so quiet, so still and attentive as to hear the voice of the Father calling us to share his love for the whole of creation. Prayer, and the doing of God's will, is to enter the realm of the Father's mercy, compassion, and desire for justice, and to be changed by the priorities of God. It is therefore also to assume, once more, our rightful place as faithful stewards who have been given authority and "dominion" over the earth. The more we become familiar with the One whom Jesus called "Father," and the more we understand all that God has done for us in Christ, the more we will have a sense of how to pray, what to ask for, and what to avoid.

If prayer is first listening and only second speaking out what we have heard, it will also involve, third, waiting. As with all spiritual gifts and their exercise, prayer will always be partial and imperfect for the time being, always looking forward to a fulfillment yet to come. Viewed in this light, the problem of unanswered prayer is not so much one of wondering, "Where is the graciousness of God?" or "Why does God not care?" as it is of crying out, "How long, O Lord?" Even the answers that we do receive, however

---

10. Julian of Norwich, *Revelations of Divine Love*, §41, 92.
11. St. Jean, *Until the Day Breaks*, 206.

rich, will still fall short of the glory that is yet to be revealed (Rom 8:18). One way or another, we will remain acutely conscious of the injustice and sorrow that called forth our prayer in the first place.

Conclusion: Learning to Pray

Because it commences with the character of God and intentionally conforms to the will of God, our prayers will always be in response to the ways of God, even if their immediate occasion is that of a world very far from God. In this way, our prayers reflect the ministry of Jesus, whom God sent into the world, as John famously reminds us, "not to condemn the world, but in order that the world might be saved through him" (John 3:17). Again, however counterintuitive it may seem, prayer is not so much an attempt to solicit answers from God as it is a process whereby God solicits our requests in answer to his own insistence on mercy and grace. That is why learning to pray will always involve learning more about the One to whom we pray, even as we confess that for now we only "know in part" and do not yet see God "face to face" (1 Cor 13:12). Insofar as prayer, like faith and faithfulness, is always conducted with imperfect knowledge and in partial ignorance of God's ways, it must also entail mystery and a measure of uncertainty. We do not see the whole picture as God does, but we pray anyway on the basis of what we do see, trusting that in the process, we will come to see and understand more fully. Or to be more precise, while we do not yet see all things in submission or subjection to him, "we do see Jesus" (Heb 2:9), and so pray accordingly.

Viewed from a missional perspective, then, prayer involves us directly in God's own mission, whatever actual words or methods we may choose. More particularly, the fact that we are his followers means that our prayers bind us ever more closely to Jesus himself, and to *his* fulfillment of his Father's mission. The more we pray, the more we discover that it is Jesus who makes prayer possible in the first place. In other words, we first learn to pray *like Jesus*, no doubt beginning with the prayer that he taught his earliest disciples. We then learn to pray *with Jesus*, joining him in his unending prayer for us and all the world. And, finally, we learn to pray *in Jesus*, in union with him, "beholding the glory of the Lord [and] being changed into his likeness from one degree of glory to another" (2 Cor 3:18, RSV).

Bibliography

À Kempis, Thomas. *The Imitation of Christ: A New Reading of the 1441 Latin Manuscript by William C. Creasy.* 2nd ed. Macon: Mercer University Press, 2007.

Barth, Karl. *Prayer and Preaching.* Translated by Sara F. Terrien and B. E. Hooke. London: SCM, 1964.

The Book of Common Prayer. Toronto: Anglican Book Centre, 1962.

Foster, Richard J. *Prayer: Finding the Heart's True Home.* New York: HarperSanFrancisco, 1992.

Julian of Norwich. *Revelations of Divine Love.* Translated by Barry Windeatt. Oxford World's Classics. Oxford: Oxford University Press, 2015.

A Manual of Eastern Orthodox Prayers. London: SPCK for the Fellowship of St. Alban and St. Sergius, 1945.

St. Jean, Patricia. *Until the Day Breaks: The Life and Work of Lilias Trotter, Pioneer Missionary to Muslim North Africa.* Bromley, Kent: OM Publishing, 1990.

Westcott, Brooke Foss. *The Epistle to the Hebrews: The Greek Text with Notes and Essays.* Grand Rapids: Eerdmans, 1977 (1892).

Chapter 4

Being Equipped for Every Good Work

Scripture Study and the Missio Dei

———————————————————————— Seán McGuire

> All scripture is inspired by God and is useful for teaching, for reproof, for correction, and for training in righteousness, so that everyone who belongs to God may be proficient, equipped for every good work. (2 Tim 3:16–17)

The above passage is, perhaps, the most well-known and regularly quoted verse about the Bible, often pointed to as the basis for the doctrine of Scripture's inspiration. However, do Christians today believe it? Indeed, the passage explicitly points to scriptural engagement as directly tied to "every good work" we do, which certainly includes mission. Yet, when the church talks about mission, we often focus on doing things rather than on the spiritual foundations of mission, which includes studying the Bible. We may publicly confess the importance of studying Scripture, but our actions don't always match our words. A recent survey revealed that 75 percent of Canadians who self-identify as Christian, and one in three evangelicals in particular, seldom to never read Scripture.[1] Statistics such as these should strike Christians as disturbing, but not because of any religious shame that one might associate with not checking off the "Bible reading" box on their spiritual discipline checklist. No, statistics like these should disturb us because it is primarily through Scripture that God teaches us how to live as kingdom citizens, convicts us of our sin,

---

1. Hiemstra, *Confidence*, 10.

makes our paths straight, and trains us in righteousness. In this way we can participate in the *missio Dei* (mission of God).

Importantly, if we are not spending time reading Scripture, we are certainly not spending time studying it—focusing our attention and taking deep dives into what God's Word says (and means). Many have bought into the lie that study belongs to scholars alone, and that the Bible is too complex for most Christians. However, this misunderstands the nature of this discipline and perpetuates an underlying belief that study is about acquiring knowledge for knowledge's sake. Quite the opposite: Christians should study Scripture to better know its Divine Author, who continues to speak through the Bible today. As we examine God's Word, we come to know that author, are drawn deeper into relationship, and through relationship deeper into our calling as believers.

This chapter offers a theoretical and theological foundation for understanding the discipline of study and how a discipline of studying the Bible specifically leads us into mission. Although I will not focus on the "how" of study,[2] I will describe the basics of what it entails before expanding our vision of why study is essential. I argue that the discipline of Scripture study is an invitation into deeper relationship with Christ and deeper involvement in God's mission. Indeed, by ignoring the study of God's Word, we stunt our capacities to know God and to go with him into the world to build his kingdom. If we are to love the Lord our God with all our being, we need to recapture what it means to love God with our minds through the discipline of study, taking every thought captive to Christ (2 Cor 10:5) and being transformed by the renewal of our minds (Rom 12:2).

Bringing Our Thoughts to Completion: Understanding Study

Before fleshing out a theological vision for Scripture study, it is worthwhile to reflect on why study is a practical discipline in the first place. Doing this will equip us to describe what makes Scripture study a *spiritual* discipline and enable us to reflect on how study helps us participate in God's mission. As outlined in the introduction to this volume, spiritual disciplines have certain defining characteristics. They invite us to be aware

---

2. Some recommended resources for more detailed "how-to" guidance include: Foster, *Celebration*; Fee and Stewart, *How to Read the Bible*; Wilkin, *Women of the Word*; McCaulley, *Reading While Black*.

of God and better aware of ourselves, and to cultivate Christ-centered identity and community.

Studying the Bible certainly meets each of these characteristics: as we study it, we become aware of God's work in our lives and our need for a Savior. God then uses Scripture to cultivate our identity by renewing our mind in Christ Jesus, helping us further understand the Bible's message and precepts, and drawing us into God's new covenant community, the church.[3] As Richard Foster argues, spiritual disciplines are meant to transform, and the discipline of Scripture study is meant to train and transform our mind, filling it with the beauty of God's revelation.[4] By studying (and, necessarily, interpreting) Scripture, seeking to hear the voice of the Divine Author and submitting one's life to that voice, Christians are increasingly refined into Christlike individuals. "Nothing is more fundamental to the Christian life than reading the text of Scripture and submitting one's life to the One who speaks his Word through the human words of the inspired text."[5] As we study these words, the Holy Spirit illuminates our minds to understand its message and helps us to discern how best to submit ourselves to the Divine Author of the text.

Although many of us have participated in Bible studies, we may think that the kind of study requiring focused attention and "deep dives" is something only "academic" people can do. I believe that this kind of study is a spiritual discipline to be done by all Christians. We often sell ourselves short, thinking that we are not able to focus on the Bible in an intentional way for long periods. This makes us hesitate and often leaves us doing the bare minimum of Scripture engagement. Surely, we say to ourselves, *I could never study the Bible for four, five, or more hours at a time in order to understand it deeply . . . could I?*

However, throughout our lives we study and have our minds discipled by that which we study in countless ways. How many of us can give in-depth descriptions of cinematic universes such as Marvel or Star Wars—knowing not just plot points but character histories, potential story lines, and the difference between "canon" and "non-canon" details in the franchise's storytelling? Or how many are able to give a basic statistical analysis of our favorite sports teams? In any given season, I will know statistical details for multiple players on the greatest team in the

---

3. Graves, *Inspiration and Interpretation*, 43; Putman, *When Doctrine Divides*, 62.
4. Foster, *Celebration*, 55.
5. Carter, *Interpreting Scripture*, 32.

NHL (the Montreal Canadiens!) as well as the salary cap situation for teams around the league. Such knowledge only comes by regularly focusing attention on these topics and allowing it to train our minds into treating the information as important—in short, through study. Let's not kid ourselves: we study regularly, and much of it is infinitely less meaningful than Scripture is and should be to us.

Thinking through Study as a Spiritual Discipline

Richard Foster's general description of study is helpful for understanding both how we tend to study and how we can then approach it as a spiritual discipline. In *Celebration of Discipline,* Foster describes study as involving four necessary aspects: repetition, concentration, comprehension, and reflection.[6] By being repetitive, attending to something in a similar way repeatedly over time, we build habits of thought that train our minds to think in particular ways and enable us to retain the information being studied. Through concentration, the object of our study becomes our sole focus for a set-apart period of time. As we focus, we begin to understand what we are studying, and through comprehension we are able to apply insights gleaned from our study into everyday life. Finally, through reflection we come to understand the significance of what we are studying.[7] Study is not about the information we gather *per se,* but about reflecting on that information so we can move toward understanding, applying the insights of our study in our life and the life of our local church.

Reading this description of study, you may be reminded of school—copying notes, memorizing information, and taking tests to quiz you on how much knowledge you have gained. If this is the only experience we have with study, we will invariably bring this expectation to how we engage Scripture. I dreaded studying for tests growing up (so much so that I rarely, in fact, did it). Rather than memorize how calculus equations functioned, I would hike through the beautiful Northern Ontario forests just outside the doorsteps of my childhood home, studying the trails and where they led. Studying the Bible as a discipline can sometimes feel like studying for calculus, yet it is in fact so much better. The Bible is, after all, living and active, which means, as the popular saying goes, that as you read it, it reads you. The aim of this spiritual discipline is to gain

---

6. Foster, *Celebration,* 56–57.
7. Foster, *Celebration,* 57.

knowledge and wisdom that transforms our lives (Matt 7:24; Prov 2:6; Prov 9:10; Eph 1:16–19; Col 3:16). Studying Scripture should quicken our hearts, sharpen our minds, and—as we will talk about—draw us closer to Christ and God's kingdom coming. Personally, I did not learn this until I stopped studying Scripture to hoard information and started studying it to be drawn closer to Christ. This small pivot made the Bible come alive in a way I had not been attuned to before.

Many readers may have participated in small groups or Bible studies, whereby a group gathers regularly to concentrate on Scripture, increasing our understanding, and reflecting on what God is saying to us today. Although I think small group studies are vital for discipleship, these types of groups are not necessarily what I have in mind for discussing the spiritual discipline of Scripture study. In many evangelical churches today, group studies can be truncated into video studies that only scratch the surface of a topic, or be sermon-based studies that may build biblical literacy but do not promote the discipline of study so much as the building of community. These have their place in the church, and indeed such groups are necessary for healthy churches, if only because of the space they give for Bible-saturated communal prayer.[8] However, the theological vision of Scripture study I am proposing begins with individual commitment before extending into community. It involves being intentional about diving deeply into the biblical text on a personal level to understand its God-intended meaning, focusing on it for *hours* on end, not just forty-five minutes set aside for conversation about the Bible after a time of life check-ins.

As previously mentioned, we may assume that hours-long focused study only belongs to academic types. However, it is a disservice to ourselves and our capacities to think that we are not generally capable of this discipline. I was reminded that study was for everyone during the first week I began pastoring. Fresh out of seminary, it would have been easy to think of Scripture study in terms of exegesis only, limiting "proper" study to those with special knowledge of the biblical languages. When I walked into the church office for the first time, I noticed our church's administrator diligently working away. Wanting to get my bearings and not thinking anything of it, I did not ask her what it was she was working on at the time. A few hours later, she came to my office, booklet in hand, with all sorts of questions about the Pauline letters. It turned out that the booklet was a study guide that she would use to help her understand the Bible when

8. Lovelace, *Dynamics*, 227.

there was no other immediate work to do in the office. In spare moments, which sometimes stretched into hours, she would focus her attention on God's Word, being guided in focusing on it through these booklets so that she would better know God and grow in her love of others. Her example taught me that, if prioritized and prepared for, study can be done by anyone, with no special training required.

Through repetition, concentration, comprehension, and reflection, everyone has the capacity to study God's Word. However, there is an aspect of study that is missing—one which I think Foster failed to properly recognize and that may hold the other components together: articulation.

Thought and Speech, Word and Deed: The Importance of Articulation

When we think about articulation, we are likely to think primarily about speech—saying what is on our minds, either verbally or in written word. This is partly because of the influence of Russian psychologist Lev S. Vygotsky, who wrote about the relationship between language and thought. Vygotsky argued that our thoughts are not expressed but *brought to their completion* in our words.[9] Put another way, articulation via words is not about *expressing* but *finishing* what's on our mind and making our thoughts intelligible—to us and others. Thus, some of us find we need to work out our thoughts verbally (with others or by ourselves) before determining what we are thinking about. When we speak out loud like this, we are not testing our thoughts but finishing them, and it is only once we have finished our thoughts that we can evaluate them.

Like thoughts, study (and the theological reflections it instigates) is not completed in our thinking but in our articulation. Note that we do not communicate with spoken language alone but with actions, body language, even simple presence. The articulations of our thoughts can be expressed in how we live, sometimes in even more poignant ways than speech allows. Scripture also points us toward this with repeated instruction that connects what we think to how we live. Colossians 3:2–5 associates setting our "minds on things that are above" with putting our earthly nature to death. In Phil 4:8–9, focusing our minds on praiseworthy things is paired with putting what we have "learned, received, or heard" into practice. And 2 Cor 10:5–6 tells us that Christians demolish arguments and other barriers that inhibit

9. Vygotsky, "Thinking and Speech," 250–51.

our knowledge of God by taking every thought captive for Christ so that we would be obedient to Christ. In each of these, our thoughts, and particularly our thoughts about God, are eventually articulated in how we live, whether as rebellion against or as submission to Christ.

Study, then, should lead not just to private thoughts but to articulations, in word and deed. Indeed, a discipline of studying Scripture *without* articulation—never sharing the content of our study with others or letting it inform how we live—would mean never completing our theological reflection, and consequently never growing in Christian maturity. The aim of studying Scripture is to put what we learn into practice. Not doing so—listening but never doing—is nothing short of self-deceptive foolishness (Matt 7:24–27; Jas 1:22). This is, perhaps, one of the greatest issues hiding under the surface of the church's growing biblical illiteracy. If we each have a Bible that we can study for ourselves but also think that study is only meant for our individual benefit, confined to our "thought-life," our faith will inevitably become stunted because we never allow iron to sharpen iron by bringing our articulated thoughts and ways of living to our communities for discernment. And if we never articulate our theological reflections in word, we should hardly expect them to be articulated coherently in our deeds, because our faith is a word-and-deed faith—not one or the other, but both concurrently. Indeed, this is an inbuilt feature of the Christian faith because of the Gospel, which is a message that demands a response; a word that requires repentance and faith; and a promise whose maker is faithful for fulfillment (Mark 1:15; Acts 3:19; Heb 10:23; 1 Cor 1:9).

Thus, study as a general discipline is concerned both with the training of our minds and the shaping of our lives, leading us toward articulating thoughts in word and deed. What, then, makes the study of Scripture an explicitly spiritual discipline? It is the object of study, the revelation of the Word of God. By understanding the Bible in terms of revelation, we can begin to see how the discipline of study informs Christian spirituality and participation in the *missio Dei*.

Scripture Study, Mission, and the Knowledge of God

The Bible is a book about God. I do not think I realized this when I first became a Christian, instead falling into the habit of thinking it is a book of moral teachings, proverbs, theological abstractions, and very odd stories and songs. However, miss this insight and you will soon be missing the point—the Bible is all about God. In particular, the Bible is about a declaration that reorients all of reality: Jesus is Lord. This proposition is the heartbeat of the Gospel, and is the word that demands a response. When we hear this word, do we submit ourselves to this Lord and seek to love the triune God with all our heart, soul, strength, and *mind,* and love our neighbors as ourselves?[10] For this is the only response that glorifies God, which is the ultimate focus of the *missio Dei*.[11] If our missional activity does not lead us toward declaring the praise and prayer "to him be the glory forever" (Rom 11:36), it is likely not God's mission we are participating in. The discipline of studying God's Word helps focus our minds on how we should live to bring glory to Christ.

The Gospel's character as revelation suggests that a communication event is at the heart of Christianity. Importantly, this event is both words and Word, the message of God and the incarnation—the message that became flesh and dwelt among us. If the medium is the message, then, as Catholic media theorist Marshall McLuhan argues, "in Christ Jesus there is no distance or separation between the medium and the message: it is one case where we can say that the medium and the message are fully one and the same."[12] In Christ, word and deed together articulate the Gospel. We should not be surprised to see the Christian faith and *missio Dei* take on the same character; the church is now the body of Christ tasked with participating in his mission and ministry in the world.

Studying Scripture involves studying the words used because of our allegiance to the one who communicates using those words—doing so ensures we are able to heed what God says. As we would with a parent, spouse, child, or close friend, we show our love to others by paying close attention to what they are saying and, of course, prioritizing the relationship. We study God's Word, in our language and others (particularly the original languages) because it is God who speaks in and through the words on the page, pointing us to what John called the *logos* (Word) of God—Jesus (John 1:1, 14). The discipline of studying the Bible is meant to deepen our relationship with God and strengthen our allegiance to this *logos* as Lord. "When we speak of the Bible as the word of God, we are affirming

---

10. Jensen, *Revelation*, 39.
11. Bartholomew, "Spirituality, Mission," 33.
12. McLuhan, *Medium and the Light*, 103.

that God speaks and that we should listen."[13] And if the Bible is the Word of God, it is so because of its Divine Author.

Indeed, it is the testimony of the Word of God in print that draws us toward knowledge of the Word of God in the person of Christ. I contend that it is only through trusting the testimony of the *written* Word (which is to trust the testimony of Holy Spirit) that we can place faith in the *incarnate* Word, Jesus Christ. "The Word may be the norm for the words, but this does not compromise their right to be regarded as the authoritative, truthful and revelatory word of God."[14] It is thus possible to speak both of Jesus as well as the Bible as the Word of God, because the Spirit of our triune God inspired and speaks in and through the Bible, even today (2 Pet 1:21). To be sure, Jesus describes the Bible as the Word (logos) of God throughout the Gospels, such that refusing to refer to it in this way would be to break from how Jesus and the early church spoke of and understood God's revelation in Scripture (e.g., Mark 7:13; John 10:35; 1 Thess 2:13; Heb 4:12).

Through the discipline of study, we "hear" the message of God about the Word of God as we focus attention on the words spoken by the Father and Son and inspired by the Spirit—words that are the revelation of God's Gospel, that Jesus is Lord.[15] By studying Scripture with this revelation in mind, we are ultimately seeking to live under the relational reign of Jesus as Lord. Thus, study is not and can not just be about collecting biblical trivia or reading interesting stories but must focus on knowing the person of Christ.[16] It is this relationship that Christian spirituality names and orients us toward and is what makes Scripture study a *spiritual* discipline.

In his seminal book on renewal, *Dynamics of Spiritual Life*, Richard Lovelace reflects on the relationship between the Word in print and in the person of Jesus, saying we must depend on the inspired written Word for accurate knowledge of Christ. But he reminds us that we also depend on Christ, whose Spirit sanctifies our minds so that what we glean from the written Word is "wisdom in the biblical sense and not mere knowledge."[17] Accordingly, these two Words—print and person—have an interdependent dynamic, whereby the written Word draws us to the incarnate Word and Jesus in turn draws us back toward Scripture. And as we read, the

13. Brown, *Scripture*, 13.
14. Jensen, *Revelation*, 49.
15. Jensen, *Revelation*, 72.
16. Bartholomew, "Spirituality, Mission," 33.
17. Lovelace, *Dynamics*, 279.

Holy Spirit illuminates our mind and equips us for living wisely in our fallen world.

What, then, does study have to do with God's mission in the world? The animating feature of Scripture study as a spiritual discipline is that it helps us grow in our knowledge of God, and consequently live "lives worthy of the Lord" (Col 1:10). Simply put, the more we are drawn to Christ as Lord, the more we are drawn toward living as kingdom citizens who glorify God by bringing Christ's reign to bear in our lives and communities. And, because relational knowledge of God is central to the Bible's description of the kingdom of God, knowledge of God is also a central (if not the most important) aspect of the *missio Dei*.[18]

As we develop a deeper relationship with God, we are transformed into the image of Christ. Helland and Hjalmarson remind us, "As your knowledge of God increases, your love of him also increases, and you thereby come to know him more through *praxis*."[19] Praxis (or practice) means that knowledge of God, derived from Scripture, involves both hearing God's voice and then doing what it says. They further claim that "the substance of eternal life is to know God and Christ,"[20] which helps reorient how we understand God's kingdom. The nearness of the kingdom relates to knowing God through Christ, and it is this knowledge that ultimately orients heaven and earth. This makes the church a countercultural organization, an embassy of God's kingdom, that articulates with word and deed that Jesus is Christ and Lord. The discipline of Scripture study invites us toward this reorientation, deepening our knowledge of God in Christ so that we can be increasingly conformed to Christ from the inside out.

However, there is an obvious danger associated with the discipline of study. The Bible repeatedly instructs us to gain knowledge and wisdom (e.g., Prov 1:1–6; 2 Pet 1:5; Phil 1:9), especially knowledge of God (e.g., Prov 9:10; Ps 111:10; Job 28:28). But knowledge can inflate our egos if it is not informed, directed, and shaped by love: "Knowledge puffs up, but love builds up" (1 Cor 8:1b). If we study without concern for the object of our study (the triune God's self-revelation) nor the ends of our study (to know and love God and neighbor rightly), we can very easily fall into the trap of "always being instructed" but never able to "arrive at a knowledge of the truth" (2 Tim 3:7). This would be, and indeed is, tragic, and

---

18. Bartholomew, "Spirituality, Mission," 32–33.
19. Helland and Hjalmarson, *Missional Spirituality*, 145.
20. Helland and Hjalmarson, *Missional Spirituality*, 145.

a warning for those who might hoard information for themselves rather than being transformed by a deepening relationship with Christ. Study separated from relationship with God will lead to pride, and the more highly we think of ourselves, the more untethered from reality we will become. At its best, the discipline of study grounds us in ultimate reality through the knowledge of God in Christ, in whom "we live and move and have our being" (Acts 17:28).

Study in Practice

I witnessed the potential that studying has for completely transforming lives while visiting Lebanon a few years ago, during the height of the Syrian refugee crisis. From 1976 to 2005, Lebanon was occupied by Syria, and the Syrian army treated the Lebanese people brutally. Everyone we met had stories about family members—fathers, in particular—who were taken away by Syrian soldiers and never seen again. When Syria fell into civil war, many Syrians sought refuge in Lebanon. The people of Lebanon faced a choice: would they now treat these people as they had been treated? Christians we met all struggled with this question, informed by a deep hatred for what they had experienced over decades. Yet, in story after story, they described how they diligently studied Scripture. These disciples read passages like 2 Cor 5, Matt 5–7, and Ps 41, day after day, long into the night after a hard day's work, until the Lord transformed their hearts and minds and led them to love these neighbors who they once hated. Through the power of the Holy Spirit, the kindness these disciples showed caused enemies to be transformed into brothers and sisters as the Gospel was articulated in word and good works. Through diligent Scripture study, these disciples were drawn toward reconciliation with God and others, and as they did, God worked powerfully in their midst.

The mission of God requires us to articulate the Gospel, in word and deed, anew in each generation, finding ways to communicate its truth coherently to a world desperate for good news. Thus, to put the study of God's Word into practice, we need to set aside time regularly (repetition) to focus our attention on it (concentration), seek to understand what we read (comprehension), *articulate* our understanding via word and deed, and reflect on what we have learned about God and ourselves through the text—particularly alongside others in Christian community. By going on personal retreat days dedicated to study, collecting tools to help us grow in this discipline, and/or inviting others to study alongside us to keep us accountable to Christ's lordship, we open ourselves up to greater knowledge of God. This knowledge, which instructs "you for salvation through faith in Christ Jesus" (2 Tim 3:15), includes an invitation from God to join him on mission, proclaiming and living the message of reconciliation in Christ for our neighbors to hear, see, and then experience for themselves. Thus we can develop natural rhythms of practicing the discipline of Scripture study and engaging in mission.

Each occasion I have taken time for study, most often during quarterly retreat days, I have encountered God and had my faith reinvigorated. If I went into a day of study with questions about how the Lord would have me live, I left with renewed conviction about how and where he was leading. If I began the day feeling empty, studying Scripture has always filled me to the point of overflowing and wanting to share what the Lord had taught me with others. And if I began studying thinking I had things figured out, the Lord would quickly humble me, convict me of my sin, and lead me to the foot of the cross to receive mercy and grace.

It bears saying that the spiritual discipline of study is not limited to the Bible. Theology, which is developed by reflecting on God's revelation, especially Scripture, can also be studied. Doing so is to learn what the church has said about God, and using it to help our own articulations of faith and our understanding of God's Word today.[21] Concerns similar to those of studying the biblical text also apply to studying theology. Some people think that theological study distracts one from the real work of the Gospel (mission), stunts discipleship, and increases pride.[22] Yet, such concerns can be mitigated by ensuring that our study focuses on helping us know and love God and neighbor rightly.

Likewise, we can also study everything the Lord has made. Scripture reminds us that the revelation of God's glory permeates all that God has created: "the heavens declare the glory of God" (Ps 19:1); "Ever since the creation of the world his eternal power and divine nature, invisible though they are, have been understood and seen through the things he has made" (Rom 1:20a). Indeed, creation has a "theomorphic" quality—that is, "things

---

21. Tools such as study guides and commentaries can be helpful for increasing our comprehension of the Bible. For accessible guides, see Carson, *New Bible Commentary*; Wright, *New Testament for Everyone* series; Goldingay, *Old Testament for Everyone* series. For more in-depth theological study, see Bavinck, *Reformed Dogmatics*; Sonderegger, *Systematic Theology*.

22. Johnson, *Theology*, 20–24.

take the form they do because they are created to reveal God."²³ This is why Foster's discussion of study includes investigating nature, for example, and why Christianity was at the center of the development of the scientific tradition in the West.²⁴ Early Western scientists did not study nature to gain knowledge arbitrarily, they studied nature as an expression of worship—their work was animated by their faith.²⁵ So it is true for many today.

However, both these forms of study are secondary to the study of Scripture, not because they are less important but because it is through studying the Bible that we learn to better recognize God's handiwork elsewhere. As Lovelace argues, "biblical truth is not a compendium of all necessary knowledge, but a touchstone for testing and verifying other kinds of truth and a structure for integrating them."²⁶ Indeed, because Scripture reveals "the true nature of created reality and history,"²⁷ it is the authoritative standard by which all other claims of revelation are tested. In other words, the revelation of the Bible supersedes revelation found in other places such as creation, but this supersession does not invalidate how creation reveals God's glory and handiwork. Rather, it confirms what God has shared in the Scriptures.

Conclusion

The message of the Gospel stays the same, but the medium constantly changes—not just because of technological innovation, but because Christ's hands and feet in the world are constantly growing, shifting, changing. As we grow in Christ through the discipline of study, deepening our knowledge of God, where will God lead us, and how will we communicate his word about the Word to the world today? This is the great invitation underlying mission—a question that is as daunting as it is exciting, and one we are invited to lean into first by "leaning in" to God so we can "lean out" to others, bringing God's kingdom to bear in our lives and the lives of every person we meet. Through the discipline of Scripture study, the Lord will teach, rebuke, correct, train us, and make us wise for salvation, so that we might

---

23. Wilson, *God of All Things*, 4.
24. Foster, *Celebration*, 63–66.
25. Kaiser, "Early Christian Belief," 1.
26. Lovelace, *Dynamics*, 219.
27. Johnson, *Theology*, 13.

live righteously, articulating the Gospel in word and deed and equipped for the good works God has prepared for us to do.

Bibliography

Bartholomew, Craig. "Spirituality, Mission, and the Drama of Scripture." In *Spirituality for the Sent: Casting a New Vision for the Mission Church*, edited by Nathan Finn and Keith Whitfield, 30–53. Downers Grove, IL: InterVarsity, 2017.
Bavinck, Herman. *Reformed Dogmatics, Abridged*. Edited by John Bolt. Grand Rapids: Baker Academic, 2011.
Brown, Jeannine. *Scripture as Communication: Introducing Biblical Hermeneutics*. Grand Rapids: Baker Academic, 2007.
Carson, D. A., ed. *New Bible Commentary: 21st Century Edition*. 4th ed. Downers Grove, IL: InterVarsity, 1994.
Carter, Craig. *Interpreting Scripture with the Great Tradition: Recovering the Genius of Premodern Exegesis*. Grand Rapids: Baker Academic, 2018.
Fee, Gordon D., and Douglas K. Stuart. *How to Read the Bible for All Its Worth*. 4th ed. Grand Rapids: Zondervan, 2014.
Foster, Richard J. *Celebration of Discipline: The Path to Spiritual Growth*. San Francisco: Harper & Row, 1978.
Goldingay, John. *Old Testament for Everyone*. Vol. I–XVII. Louisville, KY: Westminster John Knox, 2010–16.
Graves, Michael. *The Inspiration and Interpretation of Scripture: What the Early Church Can Teach Us*. Grand Rapids: Eerdmans, 2014.
Helland, Roger, and Len Hjalmarson. *Missional Spirituality: Embodying God's Love from the Inside Out*. Downers Grove, IL: InterVarsity Press, 2011.
Hiemstra, Rick. *Confidence, Conversation and Community: Bible Engagement in Canada, 2013*. Toronto: Faith Today, 2014.
Jensen, Peter. *The Revelation of God*. Contours of Christian Theology. Downers Grove, IL: InterVarsity, 2002.
Johnson, Keith. *Theology as Discipleship*. Downers Grove, IL: InterVarsity, 2015.
Kaiser, Christopher. "Early Christian Belief in Creation and the Beliefs Sustaining the Modern Scientific Endeavour." In *The Blackwell Companion to Science and Christianity*, edited by J. B. Stump and Alan G. Padgett, 3–13. Oxford: Blackwell, 2012.
Lovelace, Richard. *Dynamics of Spiritual Life: An Evangelical Theology of Renewal*. Downers Grove, IL: IVP Academic, 2020.
McCaulley, Esau. *Reading While Black: African American Biblical Interpretation as an Exercise in Hope*. Grand Rapids: IVP Academic, 2020.
McLuhan, Marshall. *The Medium and the Light: Reflections on Religion*. Edited by Eric McLuhan. Eugene, OR: Wipf & Stock, 2010.
Putman, Rhyne. *When Doctrine Divides the People of God: An Evangelical Approach to Theological Diversity*. Wheaton, IL: Crossway, 2020.
Sonderegger, Katherine. *Systematic Theology*. Vol I–II. Minneapolis: Fortress, 2015–20.

Vygotsky, Lev S. "Thinking and Speech." In *The Collected Works of L. S. Vygotsky.* Vol 1, *Problems of General Psychology*, translated by Norris Minick, 37–285. New York: Plenum, 1987.

Wilkin, Jen. *Women of the Word: How to Study the Bible with Both Our Hearts and Our Minds.* 2nd ed. Wheaton, IL: Crossway, 2019.

Wilson, Andrew. *God of All Things: Rediscovering the Sacred in an Everyday World.* Grand Rapids: Zondervan Reflective, 2021.

Wright, N. T. *New Testament for Everyone.* Vol I–XVIII. Louisville: Westminster John Knox, 2001–11.

Chapter 5

Taste and See

Mindfulness as a Means to a Missional Heart

E. JANET WARREN

WHEN TRAVELLING IN MEXICO, I usually walk briskly through towns, holding my head down, and saying "*no gracias*" to anyone who tries to sell me a trinket, tour, dinner, or . . . anything actually. On one occasion, I was already a few steps past such an alleged individual when I realized guiltily that the man had only asked if I knew the time.

I suspect all of us operate in automatic mode at times. As I noted in the introduction to this volume, we live in a noisy world. Our lives are endlessly busy, and our minds constantly chatter and twitter, oscillating between past and future. But this busyness has deleterious effects for us physically, mentally, emotionally, and spiritually. We lose the natural rhythms of life. We disconnect from ourselves, others, and, most importantly, God. How often do we miss hearing his voice? How often do we miss opportunities for serving him, his creatures, and his creation? How often do we fail to give someone the time of day?

Jesus frequently challenges his disciples, "Let anyone with ears to hear listen!" (e.g., Mark 4:23). This implies that we are not especially talented in listening, that we may not always perceive reality correctly. He asks rhetorically, "Do you have eyes, and fail to see? Do you have ears, and fail to hear?" (Mark 8:18). Old Testament authors also lament the lack of awareness within God's people. Prophets even suggest that animals understand more than humans (Isa 1:3; Jer 8:9). There is clearly room for improvement in our ability to be aware of the Lord.

Closely related to this are our ongoing endeavors to follow divine commands. In response to a Pharisee's question about which commandment is the greatest, Jesus replies: "'You shall love the Lord your God with all your heart, and with all your soul, and with all your mind.' This is the greatest and first commandment. And a second is like it: 'You shall love your neighbor as yourself'" (Matt 22:37–39). This multifaceted command is as difficult for readers today as it was for the original audience. It is interesting to note the order of these commands: one follows from the other and, in fact, circularity can be discerned. It is only when we properly love God (being constantly aware of his presence with us in order to submit to him) that we can love our neighbor (as in the mission focus of this book) as ourselves (being aware of what blocks us from fully knowing and loving God, and appropriating his love for us).

In this chapter I will unpack the above sentence, with a focus on cultivating awareness of God and self so as to be more effective in our missional practices. When our lives and minds are cluttered and our senses are overloaded, we will have difficulty hearing the voice of Jesus, difficulty seeing the stranger, and difficulty tasting the goodness of God. I suggest that being free from distractions frees us to love our neighbors. Although awareness does not fit into the classic categories of spiritual disciplines, it intertwines with and/or precedes many of them. I will focus first on ourselves, our "noises," and then on how we can overcome our hindrances through sensory awareness and mindfulness. Next, I will discuss the spiritual traditions of practicing the presence of Christ. Finally, I will consider how these practices are relevant to the ministry of loving our neighbors.

Outer Shouts and Inner Doubts

I've had some days that readers may relate to. Alarm screams. Hit snooze. Hit snooze again. Go through motions of washing, dressing. Grab stuff. Search for car keys. Stumble out door. Drive car like a robot, radio blasting to mask traffic noise. Buy food at drive-through and insert into mouth. Get into the routine of work. Busy day. Another one tomorrow. Did I walk with the Lord? Did I serve him and others? Did I even live today?

Sundays can be similarly busy and noisy. Many churches, with excellent intent, offer programs and ministries for every possible demographic and interest group. Services are filled with words and music, followed by friendly chattering. When we leave, we often have tiring family commitments. This is a far cry from the abundant life that Jesus promises (John 10:10) and is perhaps more like the fragile and fragmented world in which we live.

We tend to blame our difficulties with distraction, indeed many of our problems, on our highly technical society. It is true that instant communication (beeps, pings, and rings), rather than making lives easier, has added further complications. However, distraction is not a new concern. Consider this excerpt from a classic poem written in 1911:[1]

> What is this life if, full of care,
> We have no time to stand and stare . . .
> No time to see, in broad daylight,
> Streams full of stars, like skies at night.
> No time to turn at Beauty's glance,
> And watch her feet, how they can dance . . .

Seventy years later, but still before the electronic age, well-known contemplative author Henri Nouwen wrote, "Wherever we go we are surrounded by words: words softly whispered, loudly proclaimed, or angrily screamed; . . . words to be heard, read, seen, or glanced at; words which flicker off and on, move slowly, dance, jump, or wiggle. Words, words, words! They form the floor, the walls, and the ceiling of our existence."[2]

When we are not distracted by the outside world, our own minds are silently noisy. We revisit our annoyance at the stranger who cut in front of us in line, the colleague who criticized our work, or the store clerk who was rude. We worry about unpaid bills. We fantasize about our ideal vacation. Most of us also have vocal "inner critics," often encouraged by the evil one: "no one likes me," "I'm useless at this job," "I'm a failure at being a Christian." Nouwen believes that "the greatest trap in our life is not success, popularity, or power but self-rejection. When we have come to believe in the voices that call us worthless and unlovable, then success, popularity, and power are easily perceived as attractive solutions."[3] I would add that popularity and power are usually noisy and distracting. Nouwen further notes that memories of unhappy events or actions can lead to painful emotions such as remorse, shame, and guilt. These can lead to hardened and closed hearts,

---

1. Davies, "Leisure," public domain.
2. Nouwen, *Way of the Heart*, 31.
3. Nouwen, *Life of the Beloved*, 31.

which in turn make it difficult to discern the divine presence—the One who loves and calls us his beloved.[4]

Generally, the outer shouts are more obvious, and we can choose to escape them at times. However, the inner doubts and distractions follow us everywhere, and we are often unaware of them. Paradoxically, the classic disciplines of solitude and silence, which can eliminate external noise, often have the effect of increasing the intensity of our inner noises. This is not a problem though, because it increases our self-awareness, which then allows us to better see and hear God. We will have difficulty loving the Lord with all our minds when they are directed elsewhere. However, silence and solitude are not essential for reducing obstacles in our spiritual and missional paths. Let us consider ways that we can become more aware.

Looking and Listening, Tasting and Touching

Many years ago, I attended an Alpha course, tired and hungry after a challenging day at work. The dinner was simple but nourished more than my body. The warm aromas of multiple meatloaves wrapped themselves around me, peas and carrots were colored with the original Creation Crayon, a mouthful of baked potato dissolved on my palate, and the tingle of sour cream lingered. And then there was dessert.

I don't recall the discussion that night, but I do remember this experience because it was exceptional. Years later, I recognized my experience as a mindful one. I was fully present to the meal and my senses were engaged; I experienced eating at a deeper level. This was also an example, though implicit, of Fitch's discipline of eating together; sharing in the Lord's table allows us to be fully present.[5] I have had similar experiences in more intentional ways, such as during a discernment workshop at a TrueCity conference. However, these types of experience can be extended to all areas of life.

In our noisy world, we are often disconnected from our senses. Yet the physical senses are important in Scripture. Old Testament authors use terms related to sensory perception for discerning the Lord's presence, action, and intent: "My eye has seen all this, my ear has heard and understood it" (Job 13:1); "Oh, taste and see that the Lord is good" (Ps 34:8); "Open my eyes, so that I may behold wondrous things" (Ps 119:18); "incline your

---

4. Nouwen, *Discernment*, 113–30.
5. Fitch, *Faithful Presence*, 47–67.

ear to my understanding" (Prov 5:1).[6] Sensory imagery continues in the New Testament. In his earthly ministry, Jesus was clearly observant of trees, winds, waves, and other aspects of nature. Gospel stories tell us that Christ opens the eyes of the blind both literally and metaphorically (John 9:1–41). The disciples on the road to Emmaus feel their hearts burning within (Luke 24:32) and Paul refers to the eyes of our hearts (Eph 1:18).

The church fathers, as well as Augustine and Aquinas, use the language of the spiritual senses, such as the "eyes of the mind" or the "incorporeal eye," which enable us to perceive the Divine Being.[7] However, I wonder if contemporary Christianity has lost sight of the spiritual, metaphorical, metaphysical, and even physical senses. We can know God through creation, using our vision, hearing, taste, touch, and smell. But we can also know the transcendent creator and redeemer through senses that are difficult to describe. Both types of knowledge require intention and attentiveness. There is much classic and contemporary Christian literature on how to nurture our ability to know and listen to our Lord. But let's first consider what contemporary psychology says on the subject.

The practice of therapeutic mindfulness focuses on cultivating awareness of the senses. It is related to the ordinary concept of awareness and, in clinical terms, refers to "the practice of maintaining a nonjudgmental state of heightened or complete awareness of one's thoughts, emotions, or experiences on a moment-to-moment basis."[8] It should be distinguished from mindfulness meditation, which is a structured period of intentional focus, usually lasting thirty to sixty minutes. "Ordinary" mindfulness is a state of being rather than a specific practice, described with phrases like "waking up" or "coming to our senses."

Mindfulness has roots in Buddhism but has since largely and intentionally been stripped of any religious affiliations. Psychologist Jon Kabat-Zinn brought the practice to prominence in the 1980s and developed a program called mindfulness-based stress reduction.[9] Clinical studies have shown that mindfulness improves many physical and mental health problems. It enhances learning and bodily function; it can increase

---

6. For further discussion see Avrahami, *Senses of Scripture*, esp. 65–112.

7. See various chapters in Gavrilyuk and Coakley, *Spiritual Senses*.

8. *Merriam-Webster*, s.v. "mindfulness," https://www.merriam-webster.com/dictionary/mindfulness.

9. Kabat-Zinn, *Full Catastrophe Living*, esp. 1–146.

attunement and may enhance empathy.[10] Focused awareness allows people to separate sensations, such as bodily pain and negative emotions, so they can choose how to respond to a situation, rather than reacting automatically. If people have experienced psychological trauma, mindfulness can help them recover and process memories. It also decreases the disconnect between mental and physical experiences that is common when people have undergone emotional trauma.[11]

Psychiatrist Daniel Siegel points out that when we live in automatic mode, our lives become numb, dull, and repetitive. We also often live from the "top down," basing our thoughts and actions on past experiences and narratives. Mindfulness encourages us to cultivate "bottom-up," or sensory, experience. Siegel describes three streams of awareness: direct sensory (e.g., feeling the pressure of one's feet on the ground when walking), conceptual (e.g., thinking about walking), and observational (e.g., watching oneself walk as if from a distance). We can experience all of these in mindful living. It can be challenging and awkward to develop awareness of previously automatic processes but, with practice, it becomes natural. Siegel uses the acronym COAL to describe attitudes of mindfulness: curiosity, openness, acceptance, and love.[12] Selfless awareness, or putting aside the self and its automatic modes, increases our flexibility in dealing with life situations. It also enhances our imaginative and spiritual access to knowledge.

Mindfulness exercises include belly breathing, observing one's thoughts without judgment, noting distractions or emotions but letting them float by, walking on pebbles, and walking while noting the feel of ground and air. In a body scan, one observes the physical self from head to toe, paying attention to areas of tension. The well-known raisin exercise is an example of sensory focus. One takes an ordinary raisin, observes its wrinkles and colors, feels its irregular texture, then slowly puts it into one's mouth, noting arm movements, and observing the feel and taste of it as one slowly chews.

Mindfulness is currently very popular and applied broadly. It is effective, but it has also been promoted well, and has become a commodity in the psychological marketplace. Despite common misconceptions, it is not completely new, and resonates with existential, gestalt, and body-based therapy. As mentioned, it also aligns with many religious practices,

---

10. Siegel, *Mindful Brain*, 108–33.
11. E.g., van der Kolk, *Body Keeps the Score*, esp. 210–12.
12. Siegel, *Mindful Brain*, 15.

including Christian spirituality. There is nothing mystical or magical about mindfulness; it is the simple practice of being in the present with awareness.

However, cultivating awareness is very different in Christianity compared with Buddhism and other eastern philosophies and religions. Through our faith, we do not just connect with our material bodies or "the universe" but we connect with the Spirit of God, the Spirit of Christ, the Spirit of truth and life—a tangible Spirit that transcends us but also lives within us. We are not "all one" in the "ocean" but are distinct from our creator. We do not seek "emptiness" but to be *filled* with the Spirit. We practice mindfulness as a spiritual discipline, not a therapeutic technique. We are to be still and know God (Ps 37:7; Ps 46:10), abide in Christ (John 15:1–11), live by the Spirit (Gal 5:16), and pray without ceasing (1 Thess 5:17). Furthermore, Christianity is communal, historical, and eschatological. In addition to cultivating present awareness, believers reflect on what the Lord has done for us in the past, and on the future fulfillment of his kingdom.

The "breath prayer," likely originating with the desert fathers and mothers of the fourth century, is a Christian practice that encourages bodily/sensory awareness alongside spiritual awareness. It is sometimes called the "Jesus prayer" or the "prayer of the heart," and is often related to the supplication of the tax collector: "God, be merciful to me, a sinner" (Luke 18:13). As one breathes, one says the divine name or a brief phrase, silently or aloud. It is one way to refocus our minds, pray without ceasing, and cultivate awareness of the Lord. And, as studies on mindful breathing show, it has multiple benefits.

Some people worry that mindfulness is self-centered, in contrast to biblical teaching on selflessness. I think this concern is misguided. First, mindfulness is more about being aware of one's body and one's environment—God's creations—than about being selfish. When we are alert to ourselves and our environment, we may be in a better position to serve others. Second, recall that we have the indwelling Spirit; therefore, self- and God-awareness are similar: Spirit speaks to spirit. Since God knows us better than ourselves, mindfulness can increase our awareness of God's awareness of us! Uncluttered minds may better enable us to hear the voice of the Lord and consequently follow his commands. Third, practices that enhance awareness may reveal our sins and weaknesses, things that impair our relationships with God and others. Thus, the psalmist writes, "I commune with my heart in the night; I meditate and search my spirit" (Ps 77:6) and Peter advises, "prepare your minds for action" (1 Pet 1:13). Indeed, we can hardly "take every thought captive to obey Christ" (2 Cor 10:5) if we are not aware of our thoughts to begin with.

Christian teaching encourages us to be still, to enjoy life, and to nurture knowledge of God, creation, and self. As we look and listen, taste and touch, we can better see Jesus. As we practice stillness, we can better recognize our woundedness and our need for a healer. As we employ intuition and empathy, we are better able to be in tune with our hurting world in need of a Savior. The sensory, the imaginary, and the transcendent intertwine. Indeed, cultivating awareness can exist in a positive feedback cycle: when we are less distracted by outer shouts and inner doubts, they will likely decrease. When we are fully present in each moment of time and space, we become more open to the presence of the Spirit and can better love and serve the Lord our God. Thus, mindfulness as a spiritual discipline prepares us for mission.

The concept of mindfulness, if not the word or its current psychological use, is ancient and common to many religions. In fact, there is much written in the Christian tradition about spiritual practices akin to mindfulness that may help us follow the greatest command.

"Practicing the Presence" and Living in the Present

The title of Brother Lawrence's classic book is somewhat self-explanatory: *The Practice of the Presence of God*. In his conversations and letters, this seventeenth-century Carmelite monk describes how he endeavored to practice the presence of God all day and every day, moment by moment. He found formal prayer tedious but talked with God while working in the kitchen; "The time of business . . . does not with me differ from the time of prayer."[13] Lawrence neither rushed nor loitered, but calmly and diligently completed his tasks: cooking, cleaning, and repeating. He seamlessly intertwined work and prayer. He advised his readers to think of God in images, when doing little things, at all times, all places, before sleep, and on awakening. To silently thank him and ask his guidance in all things. When thoughts stray, redirect them without recrimination. We can have faith that God always offers grace. Brother Lawrence admitted that this practice was not easy, and often wanted to quit, but did notice that acts, when repeated, can become habits.

---

13. Brother Lawrence, *Practice of the Presence*, fourth conversation.

Almost a century later, the Jesuit Jean-Pierre de Caussade wrote about "the sacrament of the present moment" and "self-abandonment to divine providence."[14] "In the state of abandonment the only rule is the duty of the present moment."[15] In words very similar to contemporary mindfulness teaching, he points out that thinking about the past leads to regret and discouragement, and thinking about the future leads to fear; therefore, we need to "leave the past to the infinite mercy of God, the future to His good Providence, and give the present wholly to His love by being faithful to His grace."[16] God's grace, through Christ, is available to us every second of the day, and if we open ourselves to it, we will receive great forgiveness and love. The Holy Spirit writes on our souls, which are light but active in receiving and following divine inspirations. Each moment, God ordains what is best and most holy for us. All activities are empty unless they are filled with God's will and Spirit. Christ is the center of our being and we are meant to center ourselves on him. This ancient writing foreshadowed the contemporary mindfulness movement, and can be used to cultivate awareness of the Lord as well as awareness of how he wants us to love others.

Two centuries later, the missionary Frank C. Laubach continued the theme of moment-by-moment attentiveness to the Lord. In his pamphlet, "The Game with Minutes," he challenges Christians to keep God in mind for at least one second of every minute of the day. In this manner we can attempt the posture of continual prayer advised in the Epistles. (A personal confession: when I first read about this, I misunderstood it to be once an hour, and even failed at that!) Laubach suggests that we ask God what he wants done each minute. This "game" is challenging; a deliberate act of the will, involving surrender and sensitivity every waking moment. It involves a passion to be like Jesus and to "respond to God as a violin responds to the bow of the master." Laubach asks, "Can I bring God back in my mind-flow every few seconds so that God shall always be in my mind as an after image, shall always be one of the elements in every concept and precept?"[17] He describes the experience of being constantly in touch with God as amazing.

---

14. This work is published under both titles and its authorship is disputed; the concept of abandonment originated with Mme Guyon, Francois Fénelon, and Francis of Sales in the seventeenth century; de Caussade, *Abandonment to Divine Providence*.

15. de Caussade, *Abandonment to Divine Providence*, 70.

16. de Caussade, *Abandonment to Divine Providence*, 110.

17. Laubach, *Letters by a Modern Mystic*, March 23, 1930. See also Laubach, *Prayer*.

Contemporary Christian authors from diverse traditions have reinforced the concepts of living in the moment and practicing the presence of God. Foster encourages paying attention to nature, really *seeing* flowers, birds, and butterflies. He includes this practice within the discipline of study as a method of learning about "nonverbal" books.[18] Foster also cites Brother Lawrence and Frank Laubach as examples of people who exemplified the discipline of worship by cultivating a sense of "holy expectancy," living with the assumption that God is always with us.[19] Elsewhere he points out that Christians often forget the (mostly unrecorded) years Jesus spent working as a carpenter. It was likely during these years of daily duty that he learned obedience, prayer, and single-minded devotion to his Father.[20] To love God with hearts and minds does not necessarily require any special spiritual practices but simply (in theory anyway!) a change in attitude and awareness.

Nouwen, referencing the story of the storm in the Sea of Galilee (Matt 14:22–33), notes the importance of being aware of the Lord in the present moment. As long as Peter kept his eyes fixed on Jesus he could walk on water. "In the midst of all the storms, he is the quiet presence, in the midst of all our doubts and fears, he is the safe dwelling place; in the midst of all our restlessness, he is our home."[21] I would add that when we are at home, present with the Lord, we are in a better position to reach out to a hurting world.

Some literature on spiritual discernment echoes mindfulness practices. Roman Catholic Mary Margaret Funk describes the practice of discernment as watching, noticing, and observing; not analyzing. She suggests that when our minds are still and peaceful, we can "hear the subtle whisper of grace and take action."[22] When we eat and drink mindfully, we experience the fruits of transcendence. When we live from a mind that is "descended into the heart, [that] still, small voice rises with grace, courage, and poise."[23] When our egos loosen their hold on us, we can enjoy our true selves—the selves made in God's image. Nouwen similarly suggests that, by cultivating attentive presence, we can better receive blessings. He also describes

18. Foster, *Celebration of Discipline*, 73–75.
19. Foster, *Celebration of Discipline*, 161–63.
20. Foster, *Streams of Living Water*, 18–21.
21. Nouwen, *Discernment*, 129.
22. Funk, *Discernment Matters*, 5.
23. Funk, *Discernment Matters*, 58.

feeling blessed by simply being with someone.[24] Evangelical Dallas Willard encourages a conversational relationship with God, characteristic of friends who walk and work together. He likens our awareness of the divine presence to the common sensation of intuitively knowing when someone is staring at us. With the Lord, there is reciprocal awareness. Willard reminds us that God is with us even when we don't sense his presence.[25] If we are in constant conversation with the Lord, we are more likely to hear his guidance with respect to loving our neighbor as ourselves.

Reformed philosopher Don Postema focuses on Sabbath rest, but does not limit the practice to one day a week. He encourages incorporating Sabbath mindfulness into daily life, such as eating slowly, savoring meals, and eating in silence on occasion. Being aware, alert, attentive, and receptive are skills we all have, and are essential for spiritual contemplation. Postema suggests that the ringing of church bells, traditionally used to call people to a worship service, can serve as a cue for us to catch our breath.[26] Perhaps more applicable in our time, we could set an alarm on our phones or use other daily routines, such as eating, as a reminder to turn the eyes of our hearts to the Lord. (I sometimes tell people to say a breath prayer every time they go to the bathroom!)

Cultivating awareness of God on a moment-to-moment basis is not easy. We remember the God who is with us and comforts us during times of trouble (e.g., Ps 23:4), but we forget the God who desires our continual attention and who opens our eyes to missional opportunities. In his time of grief, Jesus asked his disciples to sit and keep watch with him, but they disappointed him by repeatedly falling asleep (Matt 26:36–45). Simple attentiveness is often more difficult than activity. We like to be in control, we are impatient, we like distractions, we like to flee from challenges. But we are called to be mindful of God's presence every moment of every day, as we eat, walk, work, and play. We are called to pray without ceasing and to make the mundane holy. The specifics of how we do this will be different for different people; we can adapt ancient ways to suit our own lives. Practicing the presence and living in the present relate to sensory awareness: looking and listening, tasting and touching, in both physical and metaphorical manners. It helps us to love the Lord with our hearts, minds, and souls, and to love our neighbors as ourselves.

24. Nouwen, *Life of the Beloved*, 79–81.
25. Willard, *Hearing God*, 20–35, 62–68.
26. Postema, *Catch Your Breath*, esp. 20–26, 56–58.

Fixing Our Eyes ... and Loving Our Neighbor

In recent years, my near vision has declined and I now need reading glasses. Unfortunately, they have a habit of straying, hiding, and disappearing at times. Although irritating, these assistive devices are indispensable for my daily functioning, and I become more aware of this fact when they disappear. Similarly, it is often when we lose sight of Jesus that we become more aware of our need for him. But, like reading glasses (well, sort of), tools from contemporary psychology and classic Christian spirituality can help us to fix our eyes upon Jesus (Heb 12:2). In turn, such practices can improve our ability to love and serve the Lord.

Loving the Lord, and cultivating awareness of him with our physical and spiritual senses, is a prerequisite for loving our neighbors, i.e., mission. Yet often we think of mission solely in terms of programs and plans, giving and doing. Instead, we can conceive of it as cultivating incarnational attentiveness that allows us to see the world and its people through God's eyes. When our eyes are fixed on him, we can better hear him, and better understand his love for all creation. Our mission can then align with his. When we are mindful of the world around us, we can also better see exactly how our neighbors need loving. Then we can engage in mindful mission.

Judith and Ross Thompson, following a form of "Buddhist Christianity," have written about practicing mindful ministry, noting that practical aspects of awareness (the psychology of mindfulness) and theological reflection are interdependent and mutually enriching. Mindfulness offers "an unencumbered and joyous inhabiting of God's kingdom on earth in which all are invited to share."[27] They note that there is inherent tension in the relationships between self, God, and church. Prioritizing one over the others can lead to ministry that is too abstract and idealistic, too egocentric, or mindless (such as acting before praying or not considering the roots of a problem or mission goals). The Thompsons make some good points but I would argue that, although love for God, self, and others (neighbor, the church, the world) intertwine if we fix our eyes on Jesus and cultivate a conversational relationship with God, the Spirit can flow through us, and our love for self and others will naturally follow. And of course, it is the Spirit who inspires us to turn to Christ in the first place! And God is infinitely more mindful of us than we are of him. Furthermore, although we have been focusing on divine immanence, we must

---

27. Thompson and Thompson, *Mindful Ministry*, xviii.

not do so at the expense of forgetting the majestic transcendence of God, above and through all creation.

As Brother Lawrence and others point out, awareness of God does not require inactivity. We can practice the presence during our work, in the kitchen or anywhere else. We can practice the presence during our interactions with our neighbors. Being still in our minds and bodies, and being in touch with our spiritual senses are compatible with missional activities. When our spirits and wills are aligned with God's, we are better able to hear his missional call. When our eyes are fixed on his, we are better able to be his hands and feet in the world. We are to keep our minds on Christ continually as we live out our days. Practicing the presence of God is an act of worship. It aids in our own spiritual formation and enables us to better discern the need and manner of mission service. As we practice the presence, we also mediate the presence. The discipline of mindfulness can assist us in fulfilling the great command to love the Lord our God with heart, soul, and mind, and our neighbors as ourselves. It can help us develop spiritual and missional rhythms as we sing the Lord's song into our spiritually splintered world.

Mindfulness, sensory awareness, and practicing the presence of the Lord are not classic spiritual disciplines but interact with them. Disciplines, such as silence, study, and solitude, may improve our ability to live in the moment and be present to ourselves, others, and God. The practices suggested in this chapter do not require scheduling but occur moment by moment in all that we do. It is a lifestyle. Indeed, I would say that they are more than just spiritual disciplines but a necessity for every Christian. We need to move out of automatic mode, being self-aware but not self-preoccupied. We need to fix our eyes on the Lord continually so that we can see others through his eyes. How can we discern the voice of God if we do not listen? How can we know the Lord's goodness if we do not taste? How can we know his missional calling if we do not see?

Bibliography

Avrahami, Yael. *The Senses of Scripture: Sensory Perception in the Hebrew Bible*. London: T & T Clark, 2012.

Brother Lawrence. *The Practice of the Presence of God: The Best Rule of a Holy Life being Conversations and Letters of Brother Lawrence*. Grand Rapids: Christian Classics Ethereal Library, n.d. https://ccel.org/ccel/lawrence/practice/practice.

de Caussade, Jean Pierre. *Abandonment to Divine Providence.* 10th ed. Translated by E. J. Strickland. Grand Rapids: Christian Classics Ethereal Library. https://ccel.org/ccel/decaussade/abandonment/abandonment?queryID=10457410&resultID=971.

Davies, William Henry. "Leisure." In *Songs of Joy and Others*, public domain, 1911.

Fitch, David E. *Faithful Presence: Seven Disciplines that Shape the Church for Mission.* Downers Grove, IL: InterVarsity, 2016.

Foster, Richard J. *Celebration of Discipline: The Path to Spiritual Growth.* 3rd ed. New York: HarperOne, 1998.

———. *Streams of Living Water: Essential Practices from the Six Great Traditions of Christian Faith.* New York: HarperOne, 1998.

Funk, Mary Margaret. *Discernment Matters: Listening with the Ear of the Heart.* Collegeville, MN: Liturgical, 2013.

Gavrilyuk, Paul L., and Sarah Coakley, eds. *The Spiritual Senses: Perceiving God in Western Christianity.* Cambridge: Cambridge University Press, 2012.

Kabat-Zinn, Jon. *Full Catastrophe Living: Using the Wisdom of Your Body and Mind to Face Stress, Pain, and Illness.* 15th ed. New York: Bantam Dell, 2005.

Laubach, Frank C. *Letters by a Modern Mystic.* Compiled by Robert S. Laubach. London: SPCK, 2011.

———. *Prayer: The Mightiest Force in the World.* Westwood, NJ: F. H. Revell Co., 1946.

Nouwen, Henri J. M. *Discernment: Reading the Signs of Daily Life.* With M. J. Christensen and R. J. Laird. New York: HarperOne/Harper Collins, 2013.

———. *Life of the Beloved: Spiritual Living in a Secular World.* New York: Crossroads, 1992.

———. *The Way of the Heart.* New York: Ballantine, 1981.

Postema, Don. *Catch Your Breath: God's Invitation to Sabbath Rest.* Grand Rapids: CRC, 1997.

Siegel, Daniel J. *The Mindful Brain: Reflection and Attunement in the Cultivation of Well-Being.* New York: W. W. Norton, 2007.

Thompson, Judith, and Ross Thompson. *Mindful Ministry: Creative, Theological and Practical Perspectives.* London: SCM, 2012.

Van der Kolk, Bessel. *The Body Keeps the Score: Brain, Mind and Body in the Healing of Trauma.* New York: Penguin, 2015.

Willard, Dallas. *Hearing God: Developing a Conversational Relationship with God.* 4th ed. Downers Grove, IL: InterVarsity, 2012.

Chapter 6

Fire and Stars

Neighborhood Engagement as a Spiritual Discipline

— Aaron Smith

I WAS ON MY way to unlock the church for our evening prayer meeting when two children ran past me shouting, "Fire!" Running up the three flights of stairs to see if there actually was a fire, I saw a home about two hundred feet from the church that was engulfed in flames. I thought for sure it would soon reach us. After I let neighbors know, we made a quick evacuation. While I was grabbing important documents, Reymon,[1] a man I had worked closely with in my community, came over asking how he could help. Knowing he lived very close to where the fire started, I asked about his home. He replied that he was able to get his mother to safety but that his home had already caught fire before he could salvage any of his possessions. He went on to say, "Since I don't have to guard my possessions, I am free to help others evacuate."

After helping me get to safety, Reymon immediately went back into the fire zone to help others. I stood with other evacuees in the midst of the chaos thanking God for the display of sacrificial love that I had just witnessed. Here was a man whose earthly possessions were currently going up in flames and he was looking for people to help. The great pain of the fire that ended up destroying 150 homes and displacing five hundred families was balanced by the joy of seeing God work through the life of a man whom I had worked with over the years.

---

1. Names have been changed for those who desire to remain anonymous.

Neighborhood engagement is important for followers of Jesus because it is one of the ways God brings his people into a deeper fellowship with him. My experience with this has been among the urban poor in Manila, Philippines. Throughout my journey I have experienced great pains as well as great joys. During a recent sabbatical, I was able to step out of my context and reflect on how I have been impacted by my experiences. This practice helped me to realize that neighborhood engagement is a spiritual discipline. My experience has been that God uses acts of love not only to serve others, but also to bring us closer to him. I have been transformed by my ministry among the urban poor. My relationship with God has grown as a result of neighborhood engagement.

In this chapter I will present a brief overview of the spiritual discipline of neighborhood engagement, looking specifically at loving God and loving others. Next, I will focus on an overview of how neighborhood engagement works hand in hand with prayer and Bible study as a complementary spiritual discipline. Finally, I will share a brief summary of some of the major ways that such engagement leads to spiritual growth.

The Spiritual Discipline of Neighborhood Engagement

Neighborhood engagement is at the heart of what it means to be missional. It includes working to improve the quality of life in a community as well as joining needy people in their struggle to overcome poverty. Neighborhood engagement can take hundreds of different forms including, but not limited to, prayer walks, discipleship, community development, tutoring, and advocacy.[2] God has given each of us different gifts that can be used to love others. This means that everyone has something to contribute by using their God-given gifts in service of others. Pastor and community organizer Robert Linthicum writes, "The most appropriate worship of God is sometimes the service of humanity."[3]

Neighborhood engagement can be seen as comprising the small daily steps we take to address the pains of the world in Jesus's name. It includes loving the poor, oppressed, and the physically or mentally disabled. Not all followers of Jesus are called to intentional, direct neighborhood engagement with the marginalized. However, everyone who claims commitment

---

2. See my book, *Thriving in the City*, for an expanded description of neighborhood engagement.

3. Linthicum, *City of God*, 172.

to Christ is called to love those who are least loved in society. Since God is concerned for the welfare of those who are marginalized by the world, so too should his followers be.

Neighborhood engagement is a spiritual discipline in the sense that God can use our acts of love as a way to cultivate our hearts to grow us in Christ. As Janet Warren describes in the introduction to this volume, spiritual disciplines help us to be "God aware" and self-aware; these ultimately allow spiritual formation to thrive. Before moving on, we will briefly examine loving God and loving your neighbor as they relate to neighborhood engagement.

Loving God

Neighborhood engagement is one way we can obey the greatest commandment of loving God with our whole being and loving our neighbors as ourselves (Matt 22:37–40). Loving God needs to be the forefront of disciples' lives in order for us to grow deeper in our relationship with Jesus. John explained in his first Epistle how we are to love God: "that we obey his commandments" (1 John 5:3). We love God through obedience. This is not a legalistic attempt to earn favor with God, but a joyful desire to walk in fellowship with our heavenly Father.

When the pandemic caused education to shift to online, many students requested to study at my house. My family wanted to obey God's command to love others so we extended the invitation for them to regularly do their online classes at our home. Obviously, this was inconvenient, but it also added to our lockdown experience. If our motivation for welcoming students into our home to do their online classes was trying to earn bonus points with God, the experience would have quickly become burdensome. We would have ended up despising the students whenever they came over. Thankfully that did not happen. Since our motivation was to love God and truly serve the students, we ended up having many wonderful conversations, our children had extra playmates, and a college student came to faith in Jesus.

Loving God is not limited to retreats and stepping away from the realities of day-to-day life. It involves concrete actions that communicate that Jesus is truly Lord of our lives. Liberation theologian Leonardo Boff writes, "If we undertake no liberating action, then not only do we not love our neighbor, we do not love God."[4] Boff rightly equates engagement with both loving others and loving God. Faithful saints are recognized by their lives that are poured out for God by loving others.

In the initial stages of the COVID-19 pandemic, harsh lockdowns left many families in my community without an income. My church was able to provide food on a weekly basis to some of our most needy neighbors. Two men from my church regularly came with me when we bought food for distribution. On the way they noticed homeless families along the street and observed that the local government was not helping them. These two men, who recently lost their jobs and were dependent on food relief, took some of the extra that they received and distributed it to some of the homeless families in the area. I felt both joyful and challenged when they shared their experience of distributing food to homeless families.

Loving Your Neighbor

The concept of loving your neighbor as yourself originates in Leviticus 19:18. The theme of this chapter is living a holy life, which involves the Hebrews being religiously distinct from the nations around them and on being socially righteous. Being holy is not an abstract concept. It is concrete and affects how one lives in community with others. Holiness includes honoring parents and keeping the Sabbath (Lev 19:3). It is justice in courts through not showing partiality (Lev 19:15–16) and just business practices through having honest weights (Lev 19:35–36). It is also leaving part of one's harvest for the poor to gather and eat (Lev 19:9–10). Holiness is to love your neighbors through concrete acts of love that impact their lives in tangible ways.

Holiness is intertwined with social justice. In order to be holy, one must be just. For the ancient Hebrews, holiness was to be lived out in their distinctness, through their sole worship of Yahweh, and in their righteous treatment of others. For contemporary followers of Jesus, neighborhood engagement allows for concrete applications of this concept. Thus, it is in holiness that my family regularly eats meals with a group of students who face food insecurity. Sometimes my wife prepares a special meal and invites them for dinner. Other times they will come over in the evening and ask if they can eat because they have no food in their house.

---

4. Boff, *Faith on the Edge*, 86.

James calls loving your neighbor as yourself the royal law (Jas 2:8), pointing to its importance. Loving others is a vital aspect of living in faith. Spiritual disciplines can help us to grow in love for God and others. Biblical love is an action not an emotion. Loving your neighbor as yourself is not a warm fuzzy feeling in your heart. It is concrete actions that serve others.

The inner transformation brought about by faith allows us to look beyond ourselves. Paul wrote to the church in Philippi, "Do nothing from selfish ambition or conceit, but in humility regard others as better than yourselves. Let each of you look not to your own interests, but to the interests of others" (Phil 2:3–4). Loving your neighbor as yourself requires us to move beyond looking only at ourselves to looking at the needs of others. We cannot truly love others until we see them as people with valid needs. Spiritual disciplines must lead us to love others, not to self-righteousness.

Complementary Spiritual Disciplines

Neighborhood engagement is a complementary spiritual discipline. It goes hand in hand with other spiritual disciplines such as prayer and Bible study. Spiritual formation professor Jan Johnson writes: "Contemplatives make good activists. Their activity becomes focused, powerful, and sustained. Significant doers draw from a well of quietness before God."[5] Prayer shapes our engagement and engagement helps to develop our prayer life. The two are reciprocal. Engagement provides the constant reminder to pray and shapes the content of our prayers. Engagement puts names, faces, and stories behind the generic prayer of "Jesus, please help the hurting." Today I prayed, "Lord Jesus, help three-year-old Justin survive his bout with dengue fever. Guide Reymon and Allen to find employment that pays a livable wage. Protect Rose from her uncle who makes sexual advances toward her. Provide for Jomar so he can pay for his school project."

Different kinds of spiritual disciplines, those of engagement and those of abstinence,[6] work together as ways of cultivating our hearts to grow us in Christ. Neighborhood engagement, prayer, and Bible study allow for a balanced spiritual life. After years of experience in urban ministry, Randy White points out that "intentional immersion in the context of the city juxtaposed with reflection on the experiences of people in the Bible, who had to figure out what discipleship should look like in their urban context,

---

5. Johnson, *When the Soul Listens*, 166.
6. As per Dallas Willard's classification; *Spirit of Disciplines*.

yields an almost surgical form of transformation in an individual."[7] I have experienced this in the Philippines through heavily investing in relationships and being intentional in conversations. Having neighbors over for meals increased during the pandemic when the needs became overwhelming. These are perfect occasions for evangelism and informal discipleship as well as getting to know our neighbors and their hopes and dreams. Such conversations shape my prayers and personal Bible study as well as opening up the opportunity for further engagement such as helping people start micro-businesses or enroll in college. Throughout this journey my own faith is deepened as I see God work in the lives of neighbors.

Isaiah linked loving others with the spiritual discipline of fasting. He described the kind of fast that God honors as the spiritual discipline of neighborhood engagement: "Is not this the fast that I choose: to loose the bonds of injustice, to undo the thongs of the yoke, to let the oppressed go free, and to break every yoke? Is it not to share your bread with the hungry, and bring the homeless poor into your house; when you see the naked, to cover them, and not to hide yourself from your own kin" (Isa 58:6–7)? Isaiah wrote to the exiles that returned to Jerusalem and struggled to rebuild their nation. A major part of rebuilding was the restoration of the religious life of the community.

The corrupted spirituality of the people is what Isaiah was called to judge. The Israelites were in a dry season spiritually. They complained that God did not notice their fasts. They were going through the motions in their spiritual disciplines but, instead of seeking God's glory, they practiced a self-glorifying religion of rituals. Loving God with their whole being and loving their neighbors as themselves was not in their mindset.

God used Isaiah to expose what was wrong with their fasting. They were fasting so God would notice what they were doing for him, yet at the same time they oppressed the poor. Fasting by simply refraining from eating is not what God wants. Reflecting on Isa 58, Christian ministry leader and community organizer Derek Engdahl writes, "If the people wanted to seek God and be heard by him, they needed to become people who worked for justice and cared for the homeless and hungry. This, God insisted, is real spirituality."[8] Isaiah called for fasting in the form of neighborhood engagement that leads to transformation. God rejected selfish fasting. It was only when their spiritual disciplines resulted in social justice for the oppressed

---

7. White, *Encounter God in the City*, 45.
8. Engdahl, *Great Chasm*, 240.

(Isa 58:6–7) and the rebuilding of their city (Isa 58:12) that they experienced ultimate satisfaction by delighting in God (Isa 58:14).

Neighborhood engagement complements our prayers. Intercessory prayer grows our love for others and deepens our walk with Jesus. Linthicum writes, "Praying about the issues of our city, our community, and our neighborhood will have a transforming impact not only upon the social order but also upon our lives and our ministry in the city."[9] One of the ways my church responded to the massive economic need created by the pandemic was to help neighbors start micro-businesses. The more actively I worked with micro-business owners, the more I prayed for them and their businesses. Likewise, the more I prayed for the micro-business owners I worked with, the more I prayed for all of the micro-businesses in my community. That influenced me to make even more effort to shop locally and help neighborhood businesses.

Neighborhood engagement complements studying the Bible since it helps us move from reflecting on Scripture as merely an academic exercise to implementing its teachings in real life. God's Word can only be fully applied through loving your neighbor as yourself. I came home one evening and soon discovered that James, one of the guys I was meeting with for prayer and Bible study, had been arrested for picking up drugs from a supplier and delivering them to a local dealer. A group of us from church made the trip to the jail to visit him. James was terrified and cried as he shared how difficult it was. After his release we continued to meet. God used the experience as a wake-up call for James to change his life. Our Bible studies became much more interactive as he began to share his insights on the passages we were studying. He helped me to see things in Scripture I never noticed before. We both grew closer to Jesus as a result of our Bible study.

Neighborhood engagement helps to shed light on Scripture by providing another lens through which the Bible is read; a lens based on our experiences of loving others and on insights from the different participants in a study group. This helps to limit cultural blinders and gives fresh understanding of the text. Neighborhood engagement has shaped my prayers and given me a deeper understanding of Scripture.

---

9. Linthicum, *City of God*, 247–48.

Ways Neighborhood Engagement Leads to Spiritual Transformation

Spiritual disciplines transform us into God's likeness. It is only natural that the more we live out God's character in our lives, the more seriously we take the command to love our neighbors as ourselves. Neighborhood engagement functions as a spiritual discipline when it leads to spiritual growth, which is described in the introductory chapter of this volume as "becoming more fully united to Christ." The process of seeing God's work in my community has deepened my own walk with Jesus.

Neighborhood Engagement Helps Us to Grow in Love

Concrete acts of love do not mean that we *have* love. Paul taught the Christians in Corinth that good works can be done without love: "If I give away all my possessions, and if I hand over my body so that I may boast, but do not have love, I gain nothing" (1 Cor 13:3). The act of giving everything we have can be done outside of love and therefore is not the equivalent of love. I have sometimes given to beggars, not out of love, but so they would leave me alone. This is vastly different from bringing food I plan to give away and praying for God to direct me to someone whom I should give it to. Better still is when I work with neighbors in their struggle to overcome poverty such as helping them to start micro-businesses.

Spiritual disciplines should change how we view others. Loving others is a choice. We might not feel genuine love toward those around us but that should not prevent us from engaging with them. I am sometimes irritated and feel less than loving toward those in my church and community. Choosing to engage can lead to a change of heart and the growth of sincere love.

I have found myself in situations where I had loved my neighbors out of obedience, not necessarily because I felt love toward them. I came home one day to find a lot of junk scattered around my front door.[10] A new family with five young children had just moved in with our neighbor. I was convinced that their favorite game at 5:30 AM was "who can make the most noise." Both parents worked so the children were responsible for getting

---

10. In the informal settlement where I live, houses are built right next to each other and accessed by narrow walkways. My neighbor's front door and my front door are only a few feet apart.

themselves to school. Sometimes they were home all day playing, fighting, and screaming. I loved them by feeding them, and encouraging them to go to school, including on occasion walking the youngest to her kindergarten since she was in the same class as my oldest son.

One afternoon, following a particularly loud morning, all of the kids ended up coming over to play with my son Zach. I was amazed at how well they played together when they were treated nicely. Even more amazing was that my attitude toward them changed. I no longer regretted that they were my neighbors. They were children who needed love and encouragement. After a few short months they were evicted. I was actually grateful their new place was very close so that Zach could still be friends with the children and they could still attend Sunday school at our church. Over time, my engagement with my neighbors helped me to grow in love for them.

Neighborhood engagement helps us to grow in love, but only when our begrudging acts of love are done through prayers of confession as we repent over the attitude of our hearts. Through confession and receiving Jesus's forgiveness, we are free to love others. The messiness of loving those who are difficult to love forces us to continually return to Jesus in prayer and ultimately increases our faith.

Neighborhood Engagement Helps Internalize Scripture

Truth about God is mainly known through the Bible. Physical creation can also reveal general truths about God. Within the scope of general revelation, God can also reveal himself through human experience with the inspiration and guidance of the Holy Spirit. This helps "head" knowledge about Jesus become "heart" knowledge.

Peter's experience among the Gentiles helped him to fully grasp the truth that God's grace extended beyond the Jews (Acts 15:6–11). Peter personally saw Cornelius and his family receive Jesus, and the gift of the Holy Spirit poured out on them (Acts 10:34–48). Through this experience, he was able to fully realize the theological truth that God's love extends to anyone who believes in Jesus, regardless of ethnicity. We can know this concept from Scripture, but never experience it if we only worship in a homogeneous church. Like Peter, it takes seeing God's work in the lives of people different from ourselves to fully internalize this truth. I witnessed this when I lived with two very godly Burmese men, among the most prayerful people I have ever met. Their love for Jesus was obvious through their speech and actions. The Holy Spirit was clearly with these two men from tribal villages in a country ruled by a military dictatorship.

The truth that the poor are blessed (Luke 6:20) cannot be internalized while living in luxury. It takes journeying with the poor, experiencing their joys and pains as God is worshipped in the midst of their poverty. You can read about poverty, but never really understand it beyond an intellectual level. Prayer and studying the Bible with the oppressed sheds new light on poverty and gives a deeper understanding of Scripture. I recently led a Bible study on 1 John 3 with neighbors, all of whom face food insecurity. The participants reflected on loving with actions through their daily acts of generosity. They shared stories of sharing food with hungry classmates when they had extra, as well as being the beneficiary of another friend's generosity when they were in need.

Neighborhood Engagement Fights Isolation

One of the splintered spaces that we are singing into through neighborhood engagement is that of loneliness. Humans were created as social beings. We are meant to live in community. Being abandoned on deserted islands was a form of punishment for rebellious sailors during the age of exploration. Sadly, what was once punishment has become a painful daily reality for many. The word "marooned," meaning trapped on a deserted island, has fallen out of use. Yet, people maroon themselves with the perception that good neighbors are not seen or heard. When a friend just moved into his new house he went around meeting the neighbors and learning about the community. One neighbor shared that he liked where he lived because his neighbors "keep to themselves." Upon hearing this, my friend thought to himself, "Does that mean I am a bad neighbor for wanting to meet my neighbors?"

One afternoon during a short visit to the United States I was hanging out on the porch with my family when another relative came over and asked why we were "going hillbilly." Somehow the idea of sitting outside with the possibility of talking to passing neighbors has a negative connotation. Distorted ideas of what neighborhood life should look like have made modern society a lonely place to live. In order to truly love others, we must first build meaningful relationships. In this way engagement can help us to fight isolation in our own lives. Neighborhood engagement forces us to get out and challenge cultural norms that encourage people to maroon themselves from healthy social interactions.

Neighborhood Engagement Leads to Sovereign Encounters with Others

God can use our acts of love for others to be mutually beneficial. It is helpful to ask, "What can be taken back to God in prayer based on this encounter?" John Perkins, well known for his work in Christian community development, writes, "We need to be willing to let God teach us, encourage us, and reveal his love to us anew from the people we want to serve."[11] One biblical example is that of Philip and the first African follower of Jesus (Acts 8:26–40). God directed Philip to a particular road where he saw an Ethiopian riding in a chariot. Then the Spirit told Philip to go to the chariot. Philip obeyed and when he ran up to the chariot he heard the Ethiopian reading from Isaiah. Philip joined him in the chariot and explained to him from Scripture the good news about Jesus. The Ethiopian was baptized and went home rejoicing. Philip's encounter was fully directed by God. Philip was also obedient in the matter and was able to experience the joy of a God-centered conversation that led the Ethiopian to receive Christ.

Neighborhood engagement puts us in a place where we can have sovereign encounters with others when we are intentional and sensitive to the guidance of the Holy Spirit. My experience with Adam, a mentally disabled young man in my community, illustrates this. His speech problems are so severe that he can only make grunting sounds. He smells like he rarely bathes, and his clothes are often in rags. One afternoon a group of guys from the neighborhood were gathered around Adam laughing hysterically as he was attempting to do cartwheels on gravel. Poor Adam did not have much coordination so his meager attempts were great entertainment for the onlookers.

After seeing Adam grimace in pain as the gravel scraped his hands, and hearing the roar of laughter from the guys, I felt convicted to respond. I walked into the middle of the group of rough-looking men and politely said, "That's enough. He's already hurting." They replied, "Sorry pastor, we're just having fun." I knew most of them and they respected me enough to listen to my request. Adam held his hurting hands and walked away. But he began treating me differently after that incident. He greets me with

11. Perkins, *Beyond Charity*, 63.

a grunt when we see each other. If he is behind me he will tap me on the shoulder and wave hello. He regularly passes my house and stops to smile and wave. I have no way of knowing how much of an impact I have had on Adam's life. We have never had a verbal conversation, but we do share friendly exchanges that are obviously meaningful for him. Knowing Adam helps me to see God's goodness and my own limitations more clearly. I have no ability to communicate with Adam other than a wave and a smile. Through these limited actions, God is present. I have grown closer to Jesus through seeking to love Adam.

Conclusion: Seeing the Stars

My experience in the Philippines has shown me what it means to love your neighbor as yourself. My faith in Jesus has deepened as a result. Practicing neighborhood engagement as a spiritual discipline is an important way for us to grow deeper in our faith in Jesus. Neighborhood engagement involves an intersection between missional activity and spiritual formation. It is missional in the sense that it is a concrete expression of God's love in a hurting and splintered world. It is a spiritual discipline in the sense that the Holy Spirit uses neighborhood engagement to transform our lives in Christlikeness.

Neighborhood engagement has challenged my faith as I witnessed the love and faithfulness of others. The first day after a fire destroyed much of my community was spent in cleanup. All of Reymon's possessions were swept into a charred pile of debris in the corner of what was left of his house. By evening the community was pitch black because the electric lines were all burned. Reymon lay down in his roofless house and noticed that he could see the stars. The sadness of the day was replaced by the joy of seeing the beauty of the stars. Reymon praised God for being able to see the stars, more of his creation than ever before in our community, before drifting off to sleep. When destructive fire leaves painful splintered spaces, there are surprising stars that sing joy into it.

Bibliography

Boff, Leonardo. *Faith on the Edge: Religion and Marginalized Existence*. Translated by Robert R. Barr. Eugene, OR: Wipf & Stock, 2011.

Engdahl, Derek. *The Great Chasm: How to Stop Our Wealth from Separating Us from the Poor and God*. Pomona, CA: Servant Partners, 2015.

Johnson, Jan. *When the Soul Listens: Finding Rest and Direction in Contemplative Prayer*. 2nd ed. Colorado Springs: NavPress, 2017.

Linthicum, Robert. *City of God, City of Satan: A Biblical Theology of the Urban Church*. Grand Rapids: Zondervan, 1991.

Perkins, John. *Beyond Charity: The Call to Christian Community Development*. Grand Rapids: Baker, 1993.

Smith, Aaron. *Thriving in the City: A Guide for Sustainable Incarnational Ministry among the Urban Poor*. Pomona, CA: Servant Partners, 2015.

White, Randy. *Encounter God in the City: Onramps to Personal and Community Transformation*. Downers Grove, IL: InterVarsity, 2006.

Willard, Dallas. *The Spirit of Disciplines: Understanding How God Changes Lives*. San Francisco: Harper & Row, 1988.

Chapter 7

Loitering with Intent

Hospitality, Prayer, and Encountering the Other

 Jill Weber

It's in the back of a moving van that I most feel like a monk. More of a monastic really. If we're going to get technical, I'm probably closer to a friar: a type of monastic who is embedded on the front lines of urban mission in our city rather than one who is tucked away behind the cloister wall.

It's July. Which means it's hot. In an alley in downtown Hamilton, surrounded by a sea of concrete, the truck shimmers in the heat. Perhaps it's a mirage. Perhaps an oasis. We hope it's the latter. We're stocked with water. The storage area in the back of the truck is set up as a combination living room, art workshop, and sacred space. The walls are papered with newsprint and scrawled with prayers written by passersby. A bedraggled and stained carpet covers the floor. Large throw pillows are scattered around the "room's" edges. We call it the "Prayer Truck." The cargo door of the truck is open to the street and on the sidewalk is a simple sign that says, "Need Prayer?" From seven in the morning until midnight, we sit in the truck and wait. We keep things simple. Simple hospitality. Simple listening. Simple prayer.

In the early morning, people are usually on the way to work, parking their cars in the lots that surround the truck, and scuttling off to whatever office awaits them. As they hustle past they duck their heads and avert their eyes. Or they are bowed toward their phones (another kind of morning devotion, perhaps?), scrolling one-handed as they walk. We smile and breathe a silent prayer for them as they go but let them be. Others look at the sign, look at us. Do a double take. They reach for us with their eyes. Some hesitate. Others stare gape-mouthed.

Neighborhood friends like Jackie pop by for a chat. As she tucks herself into the shade of our umbrella, her chihuahua perches in the front basket of her walker, panting and trembling. "Can you give him some water? He's really hot. Maybe squirt him?" We keep a spray bottle handy to mist ourselves down when the heat gets overwhelming. Somehow the spritzing encounter takes sacramental shape in Jackie's mind. "Make sure you bring your pets to the Prayer Truck!" She announces to passersby. "They baptize dogs there!"

Friends and strangers come for water. Sometimes they come for prayer. Mostly they come to talk. A young man, heavily tattooed and sleeveless in a leather vest, perches on the edge of the truck. He's talking but not looking at me—eyes diverted to the doodle he's drawing on the wall. Words drip from his mouth like a leaky tap, but then as he senses space and safety, they begin to flow more freely. What pours out are almost unbelievable stories of childhood neglect and vicious abuse. How, many years later, he crawled back from the precipice of self-destructiveness and despair. As he tells his story, he gathers the shards of his shattered life, trying to see how they fit back together. All the while drawing. Story done, he swaggers off, leaving behind him his doodle—a Celtic cross surrounded by whorls and knots. Arching over it are the words "God works in mysterious ways."

For the last sixteen years I've brought leadership to an urban mission's base, or new monastic community, called the Greater Ontario House of Prayer. Our primary area of focus is a vulnerable but resilient community. It's in the east end of Hamilton, Ontario, an industrial city that lost its industry years ago, crumbling into disrepair and despair. In that neighborhood we live, pray, work, and play, seeking to incarnate the presence of Jesus.

Years ago, a Benedictine friend wrapped a pithy phrase around our intention: "We are the loving presence of a people of prayer." As we've sought to live the way Jesus lived, I've become increasingly both compelled and informed by Jesus's assertions about how he navigated life and vocation. How did he wade through the weight of expectation and the grueling demands of ministry? I believe that John 5:19 gives us some insight into his modus operandi: "Jesus said to them, 'Very truly, I tell you, the Son can do nothing on his own, but only what he sees the Father doing; for whatever the Father does, the Son does likewise.'" He can do only what he sees his Father doing. I find that word "only" confrontational and disturbing. What would it look like for us to do only what we see the Father doing? With that as the criteria, how much would get culled from our calendars? And how on earth do we see what the Father is doing anyway? How do we cultivate Jesus's way of seeing? How do we grow in discernment?

Ruth Haley Barton defines discernment in a general sense as "the capacity to recognize and respond to the presence and the activity of God—both in the ordinary moments and in the larger decisions of our lives."[1] When we cultivate the habit of discernment every human encounter holds the possibility of divine encounter. The questions we must ask ourselves, and which I address in this chapter, are: How do we create space for encounter? How do we recognize encounter when it comes, particularly when it is disguised as interruption? How do we receive the gift of the moment and the gift of the other? How do the missional practices and spiritual disciplines of availability, hospitality, and contemplation put us into the path of oncoming grace?

Creating Space

Our Prayer Truck methodology is simple. We create space—a physical prayer space and temporal space in our day. We invite God to come and fill that space in any way that pleases him. And then we wait, expectant, curious, eyes wide open. During the first year of Prayer Truck, passersby were both confused and bemused: "Are you guys a hippie truck? Do you live here? Can we live here? D'you want some weed?" As we continued year after year, word got out in the neighborhood. Prayer Truck became a fixture, a gathering place the locals looked forward to with anticipation. Over the course of the month a curious community (whom I affectionately called the posse) congregated around the truck each evening.

I love taking the first shift of the season. I arrive early and roll up the back door of the truck. Set out a couple lawn chairs and a patio umbrella that shields us a bit from the unrelenting sun. Put out the sign. This year as I'm setting up, a young man runs toward me across the parking lot. He is rolling a bike and perched on the bike is a large portable toilet that looks like it had been nipped from some elderly man's bedside. "Prayer lady! Thank God you're here!"

I remember him from several years ago. A self-confessed pimp who wrote a prayer on the truck wall, asking God for a new line of work

1. Barton, *Pursuing God's Will*, 10.

because he had fallen in love with one of his "girlfriends" and wanted to marry her. This year his baseball cap is still jauntily perched backwards on his head, but he looks like he has fallen on harder times. His face is leaner, gaunt and pocked. Bedbug bites scab his arms. He leans his laden bike against the side of the truck and settles down to chat. "The crystal meth is just killin' me, effin' grinding me down. But I'm having these experiences. Weird, like kinda God experiences. He's talking to me and I don't know what the eff to do. . . . "

Sidewalk confessionals with local pimps who are encountering God. It's always amazing what can happen when we create some space. However, the challenge for those of us who are missionally minded is that most of us don't have space. The needs around us are great. Utterly overwhelming, actually. The brokenness of the world and our unique context far outstrips our meager resources. Our calendars are full and most of us (if we are honest) are running tired. How on earth are we going to find space?

And if we could find space, why on earth would we? When the tumult dies down and we are left in silence and stillness, most of us (if we are honest) get a bit twitchy. We are uncomfortable in our own skin. We are keenly aware that if we are not fighting battles without, we might have to address the monsters within. Barton says: "We all come into solitude holding a lot; cares and concerns about our responsibilities, fear and uncertainty about the experience of solitude itself, longing, and desire. The fact that we are holding so much and don't know what to do with it all can sabotage our efforts to enter in."[2]

Space, solitude, and stillness open the door to the abyss. The wound. The gaping maw within us that hungers and demands to be fed. Thomas Merton calls it our "existential dread."[3] Space stretches outward and inward into infinity, and we are unprepared for the journey. So instead, we stay home puttering about among the familiarity of busyness and distraction, trying to fill the emptiness. But if we can bear it, if we can stand it, we can step into the space . . . and wait.

Interruption or Encounter?

If we're allergic to space, then we have an anaphylactic response to interruption. There is nothing more likely to illicit irritation and aggravation than

---

2. Barton, *Invitation to Solitude and Silence*, 344.
3. Merton, *Climate of Monastic Prayer*, 213.

when, as Robbie Burns says, "The best laid schemes o' mice an' men gang aft agley."[4] We have goals. We know where we are going and how to get there. And we are on our way. Just like Peter and John were in Acts 3:1–10:

> One day Peter and John were going up to the temple at the hour of prayer, at three o'clock in the afternoon. And a man lame from birth was being carried in. People would lay him daily at the gate of the temple called the Beautiful Gate so that he could ask for alms from those entering the temple. When he saw Peter and John about to go into the temple, he asked them for alms. Peter looked intently at him, as did John, and said, "Look at us." And he fixed his attention on them, expecting to receive something from them. But Peter said, "I have no silver or gold, but what I have I give you; in the name of Jesus Christ of Nazareth, stand up and walk." And he took him by the right hand and raised him up; and immediately his feet and ankles were made strong. Jumping up, he stood and began to walk, and he entered the temple with them, walking and leaping and praising God. All the people saw him walking and praising God, and they recognized him as the one who used to sit and ask for alms at the Beautiful Gate of the temple; and they were filled with wonder and amazement at what had happened to him.

Peter and John were heading to their daily scheduled prayer time. On the way, they are confronted by a panhandler. An interruption. A spoke in their wheels, a glitch in their program. They seem unfazed. Could it be that they understood, after three years with the Master (whose ministry it seems was comprised almost exclusively of interruptions) that the interruption was the work, the divine appointment, the moment of encounter? They receive the interruption as divine invitation. They stop. They look. What might the Father be doing here?

Encountering the Other

Robert is a Catholic deacon in Toronto. He has the most engaging elfin smile I've ever seen. His white shock of hair tufts on top of his head, matching the clerical collar he wears. He's Scottish and when he speaks in a delightful brogue, words skip and flip off his tongue like children on a playground. Several years ago, I heard Robert speak at a local Catholic parish. Maybe it's my

---

4. Burns, "To a Mouse."

own Scottish heritage (my grandmother was a Macleod!), but I could listen, enthralled, to someone reading a grocery list in a Scottish accent.

It wasn't a grocery list he was sharing, but rather the story of his weekly walks. Robert "prayer walks" the red-light districts in Toronto every Thursday night. He's a fixture now. The locals know he's not looking for some company in the way they would normally expect. He walks. He prays. He is present and expectant. He shares his wisdom with me: "Every human interaction becomes either one or two things: exploitation or contemplation. You are either entering an interaction in order to make something happen, to convince someone of something, to achieve your own ends. Or you are entering the conversation to be present, to be full of wonder, to receive the other." I will never forget his beatific smile or those words. They caused me to re-examine the nature of my interactions with those around me.

I wonder though if there is another marker between those two endpoints of the human interaction continuum, between exploitation and contemplation. I would like to suggest we add something in the middle, something that I will call "transaction." In exploitation we are trying to dominate, to assert our own will, to objectify others and use them for our own purposes, regardless of how it impacts their well-being. This doesn't have to be as extreme as prostitution. It can be far more subtle. In transaction, our interchange is primarily functional, purpose driven. I want something. You need something. I am a service provider. You are a recipient of my services. Perhaps I have a rattle in my car, and you are an auto mechanic. Perhaps I am an accountant, and you need your taxes done. We are doing something together. The elements of selfishness and misuse are absent (mostly, we hope), and one can indeed transact in a loving manner, but the interaction is primarily shaped by task, functionality, and expediency. On a side note, the increasing trend of messaging or texting as a primary means of communication has moved our human interactions primarily into the realm of transaction. We don't text just to shoot the breeze, to enjoy being with one another. Text messages are usually succinct and to the point. "On my way!" "See you later!"

In a contemplative interaction, however, we are simply present to encounter the other. We receive the gift of the moment, the gift of the other, and the gift of the Divine Other. In encounter, the veil is torn between the temporal and the eternal, and barriers between us and others are torn down as well. Encounter is a moment of holy interchange, the moment we are longing for when we pray "let your kingdom come." In

Acts 3:1–10, the beggar at the temple courts is aiming at transaction. He asks for money. He's got nothing to give in return, except maybe the offer of religious brownie points or the "feel good" of helping the poor. Instead, the beggar receives divine encounter. His life is radically changed, way beyond a mere transaction.

The temptation of defaulting to mere functionality in relationships is familiar for those of us who live and work with those on the margins. My friend Aaron White and his family have lived for two decades in the poorest slum in Canada—the Downtown East Side of Vancouver. It is six blocks by six blocks and crammed full of about ten thousand addicts, although numbers are decreasing due to gentrification and the horrific numbers of opioid overdoses. "I don't usually give out money or food on the street," Aaron says. "Lots of groups already do that, but I live here, and these are my neighbors. If I am always handing stuff out, then that becomes the foundation of my relationships. Which is why I prefer inviting people to my home for dinner or finding some other way to have a generous and genuine human interaction."

Transaction is quick and easy. It doesn't ask much of us or cost us that much. Encounter requires much more of us. Aaron's invitation to dinner is the invitation to encounter.

The Gift of Wonder

In the story in Acts, Luke says that Peter looks straight at the beggar, as does John. Why did he include this observation? Let's think for a second about our reactions when our personal space, time, and agendas are intruded upon. We are driving and stop at a red light. In my neighborhood there are often panhandlers who work the line of cars while they wait for the light to turn. What do we do? Do we make eye contact? Look away? And if we are with a friend in the car, do we both give the beggar our full attention, or is it easier to turn our conversation and attention to one another and exclude the one who is breaking into our relational space, the interloper?

Peter and John respond differently than many of us would in that moment. "Peter looked straight at him as did John," the passage says. I love the mutual looking. Peter and John look straight at him. And Peter commands the man to look back at them. They contemplate one another. The word contemplate means to look at or view with continued attention; to observe or study thoughtfully. It also means to consider thoroughly; to think fully or deeply about.[5] Here is what Trappist monk Thomas Merton says:

> Contemplation is the highest expression of man's intellectual and spiritual life. . . . It is spiritual wonder. It is spontaneous awe at the sacredness of life, of being. It is a vivid realization of the fact that life and being in us proceed from an invisible, transcendent and infinitely abundant source. Contemplation is, above all, awareness of the reality of that source.[6]

Why do Peter and John look straight at the beggar and command him to look at them? What did they see in that shared moment? I wonder if they were practicing Jesus's way of seeing. The Son does "only what he sees the Father doing" (John 5:19). We find it so difficult these days to practice Jesus's way of seeing. What prevents us from doing so?

First, I believe we are prevented by our preoccupations. Our minds are a motel and there is a "no vacancy" sign hanging outside. We are so distracted and mentally cluttered that we cannot give good attention to anyone. How many of us, standing in line at a store, scroll through our phone rather than engage those around us?

Second, we are prevented by our posture of self-protection. We are inundated by a barrage of media, noise, technology. To survive the bombardment, we filter out the over-stimulus. We wear blinders and bear down on our goals and destination.

Third, we are prevented by our projections and prejudice. As the maxim says, "We don't see things as they are, we see them as we are." Psychologist David Benner writes of how we insulate ourselves from others and protect ourselves from their intrusion into our lives and psyches through a variety of strategies.[7] We emphasize their otherness—they are not like me. Or we project sameness—they are just like me! If you are not-like-me or just-like-me I can create classifications, attribute motives, or predict behaviors. Our other strategy, says Benner, is to create monsters and gods of the other. We either vilify or deify them, thereby creating the space that we need from the other to feel safe or at the very least undisturbed. We don't know if the other is a gift, or a threat. And it is very easy to default to the latter, just to be safe.

---

5. Dictionary.com, s.v. "contemplation," www.dictionary.com/browse/contemplation.
6. Merton, *New Seeds of Contemplation*, 1.
7. Benner, *Soulful Spirituality*, 124.

In this passage it seems that Peter and John set aside their preoccupation, their self-protection, and their projections. Peter and John look straight at the beggar. And tell him to look straight at them. And he gives them his attention. Attention is a precious commodity these days. Technology, busyness, entertainment, the demands of work, family, and civic responsibility gobble up our reserves. Can we think about giving our undivided attention, fully "presencing" ourselves to someone as a profound and generous act of love and hospitality? As a gift? How many people are generously "presenced"?

What if we were to give our full attention to another, leaving aside our preoccupations, our self-protections, and our projections, and fully give the gift of presence? I think if we did, we would learn Jesus's way of seeing, and encounter God in those moments of connection and contemplation. It is in "presencing" themselves to another, contemplating, encountering the other, that Peter and John become aware of divine presence. Divine activity. Divine possibility. And out of that awareness they say, "Silver or gold I do not have, but what I do have I give you. In the name of Jesus Christ of Nazareth, walk." Looking, and offering the gift of presence, leads to wonder. And in this instance leads to the miraculous.

Conclusion

This story massively challenges me and has implications for every encounter, human and divine. Because when it comes down to it there are no mere human encounters. If we are truly image bearers, then every human on the planet carries at least echoes of the creator's presence. What might it mean that this one, this other, is an image bearer of the Divine Other? Benedict in his rule says that all visitors should be received as Christ.[8] A millennium and a half later, Mother Theresa speaks of discerning Christ's presence in the distressing disguise of the poor.[9] How then does this perspective fill simple human encounter with divine portent? Not only is God present in every human encounter, but he is omnipresent. Immanent. He is here. With you and with me. Right now. My observation is that we've got some sense of God's transcendence. What we need to rediscover is his immanence. To be alive and awake to God's presence in the midst of the work of mission. To be attuned to his voice, to be open to his invitations as we love and serve those in

---

8. Benedict, *Rule of Benedict*, 51.
9. Mother Theresa, *Heart of the World*, 33.

our communities. It is this contemplative posture that breaks down the false dichotomies of prayer and mission, of worship and work.

Recently I was teaching on this topic at a local church, and my friend John Terpstra, who was leading the service, told this story:

> Friday we were stopped at a traffic light in Toronto and had to decide whether or not to open the car window and give some change to a bearded man holding a takeout coffee cup to all the cars waiting in line. We relented, this time, and rolled down the window. He thanked me politely, then looked in the car, saw Mary, and thanked her as well. The ice melted, and he asked, "Do you know how many people I've seen today?" "No," we responded. "Everyone I've looked at." Ha. It was a joke. We laughed. He laughed. He even apologized, as you do for a groaner, and offered to give us our change back. The light turned green, we waved and turned the corner, richer. Good enough for a Friday afternoon in traffic in Toronto. But when we arrived at our friend's house, he saw more: "Maybe your bearded man was saying that he sees everyone that he looks at, while most of the people who see him at the side of the road look right through him."

So here is the invitation. As we are on mission, can we see everyone we look at? Can we loiter with intent? Can we create space for encounter? Can we receive the gift of the Other? Can we be alive and awake to Divine Presence? Can we learn Jesus's way of seeing and can our work become infused with wonder and worship?

Bibliography

Barton, Ruth Haley. *Invitation to Solitude and Silence.* Downers Grove, IL: InterVarsity, 2004.
———. *Pursuing God's Will Together: A Discernment Practice for Leadership Groups.* Downers Grove, IL: InterVarsity, 2012.
Benedict of Nursia. *The Rule of Benedict.* London: Penguin Classics, 2008.
Benner, David. *Soulful Spirituality: Becoming Fully Alive and Deeply Human.* Grand Rapids: Brazos, 2011.
Burns, Robert. "To a Mouse on Turning Her Up in Her Nest with the Plough, November, 1785." Public domain.
Merton, Thomas. *Climate of Monastic Prayer.* Collegeville, MN: Liturgical, 2018.
———. *New Seeds of Contemplation.* New York: New Directions, 1961.
Theresa, Mother. *In the Heart of the World: Thoughts, Stories and Prayers.* Novato, CA: New World Library, 2010.

Chapter 8

Chimes of Redemption

Prayer Walking and the House of the Lord

Peter Tigchelaar

> Where the Body of Love is being formed
> broken hearts are being softened and warmed
> and the membrane grows thinner between
> these streets and the healing unseen. . . .[1]

THESE LINES CAME TO me in a flash while wandering through the Audubon Zoo in New Orleans with Miss Gracie, my little red mandolin. Keeping my ear to the ground, I was listening for the elusive *mots justes* to use as the opening lines of a mostly completed song. This was inspired by a recently acquired interest: prayer walking, a spiritual practice well suited to my particular proclivity as a minstrel.

This practice is based on verses such as Joshua 1:3 in which God promises that every place we set our foot would be given to us.[2] The March for Jesus, in which large groups of people walked city streets praying and singing praises, became an international phenomenon. (A quite explicit joining of mission and spiritual discipline!) I was involved with bringing

---

1. Tigchelaar, "Aching for Dawn."

2. Editor's note: The concept of praying while walking is intuitive and likely ancient; however, the term is associated with a charismatic/evangelical movement that began in the United Kingdom and was prominent in the 1990s. There is an underlying belief that the natural and spiritual worlds parallel each other. It thus has implications for intercession, expanding God's kingdom and overcoming evil spirits. It has been criticized for its weak biblical and theological underpinnings and lack of concern for social justice issues. E.g., Ediger, "Proto-Genesis"; Holvast, *Spiritual Mapping*.

this march to the streets of Hamilton during that period and was especially fond of Graham Kendrick's song "Let the Flame Burn Brighter (We'll Walk the Land)," which calls us to "walk for truth" and "speak out for love."[3] Interestingly, reportedly a result of communal spiritual discernment, these annual global marches were intentionally stopped in 2000.

After this, a more intentional emphasis on prayer was encouraged—a more subtle, undercover approach in place of the banners, sound trucks, and colorful balloons of a public procession. I noticed in retrospect that many new prayer movements, such as 24/7 Prayer in the UK and, in our local context, the Greater Ontario House of Prayer (GOHOP) were being birthed at that time. Through friendships made through the March for Jesus, I joined with various networks of intercessors, pastors, and leaders. One of our meeting venues was a former soft-core porn movie theater in the north end of Hamilton called the Playhouse, which had fallen into arrears and put on the market. It was soon to become the home for a Christian children's ministry called CityKidz.

Not long after the flickering, scantily clad images projected to mostly empty seats fell silent, CityKidz began running weekly programs for children in the refurbished building, and a group of us began to hold monthly worship and prayer gatherings. It wasn't lost on us that a redemptive shift was palpable in this very place. Walking the land, every step a prayer—taking church outside its traditional buildings—could it be that this seemingly foolish strategy was impacting the spiritual atmosphere of our city?

The lyrical download I received while strolling through the Audubon Zoo plugged perfectly into other lines I'd been carrying, lines shaped by how this and other remarkable shifts seemed to connect to a culmination of steps turned to prayer. As often happens for me as a songwriter, the opening lines came last, formed and informed by what's been gathered from previous wanderings:

> And where these chimes of redemption resound
> I'm waltzing mercy all through my hometown
> bearing ointment and holy wine
> pointing up at the gathering signs
> in back of the dawn where the Beloved has gone
> and with a spring in my step and fire on my breath
> I'm singing into the Aching for Dawn.[4]

3. Kendrick, "Let the Flame Burn Brighter."
4. Tigchelaar, "Aching for Dawn."

In this chapter I hope to give shape to an understanding of the relationship between the manifestation of God's presence in his house and our calling to be bearers of that presence in our communities—bearing the ointment of his indwelling glory and the holy wine of his love. This is the connection I see between spiritual disciplines and mission, the rhythm being one of an ongoing melodic flow between staying in and heading out, between stability and pilgrimage.

The Place Where Your Glory Abides

The immediate challenge we face in making a connection between God's presence in his house and our work as bearers of his presence in our communities is in how elusive and mysterious this house is. It is full of paradoxes that defy understanding even as these draw us deeper into relationship with the Lord. As a friend helpfully notes, "God's presence will be the hallmark of the house of prayer." This truth is sung in Psalm 26:8: "O Lord, I love the house in which you dwell, and the place where your glory abides."

The Psalms are particularly profuse in their reference to the house of the Lord (e.g., 23:6; 27:4; 65:4; 84:10; 122:1; 134:1). Other Old Testament passages describe God as dwelling in the wilderness tabernacle (Exod 25–28), Solomon's temple (1 Kgs 6:1–38), and the second temple (Ezra 3:8–10; 5:1, 2; 6:13–18). However, they are clear that God is not confined to buildings, as Solomon states: "But will God indeed dwell on the earth? Even heaven and the highest heaven cannot contain you, much less this house that I have built" (1 Kgs 8:27). Paul speaks about human-made structures being inadequate (Acts 17:24) and remarkably claims that, through the indwelling Spirit, we are now God's temple, with Christ as our cornerstone (e.g., 1 Cor 3:16, 17; 2 Cor 6:16; Eph 2:19–22).[5] The people of God become the house of God! His presence and glory are among us.

Hebrews describes a metaphorical "city that has foundations, whose architect and builder is God" (Heb 11:10). The church, built by God, is called to extend God's metaphorical city to our actual cities. Zechariah describes his vision in which Jerusalem is being measured, prophesying: "For I will be a wall of fire all around it, says the Lord, and I will be the

---

5. Editor's note: Other places God lives are Mount Zion (Pss 20:2; 65:1; 74:2), heaven (Pss 2:4; 53:2; 80:14), and eternity (Isa 57:15); the language and imagery is complex and fluid. For discussions on divine dwelling see Beale, *Temple and Church's Mission*; Koester, *Dwelling of God*; Fee, *God's Empowering Presence*.

glory within it" (Zech 2:5). God's glory that abides in his house, as in Psalm 26:8, also dwells in his city. The TrueCity network of churches in Hamilton draws inspiration from this description.

True House/False House

But how do we know if we are really living in and expanding God's house? If we are *being* the true city? The imagery of the false versus the true self can be useful for discerning whether the Lord is in fact building the house—or whether we are laboring in vain on some other building project. Perhaps a false house corresponds to the pretentious, people-pleasing impulses of a false self, and a true house corresponds to "the new self, created according to the likeness of God in true righteousness and holiness" (Eph 4:24).

The story in Second Samuel 7 relating David's desire to build a house for God is instructive for understanding this false house/true house dynamic. His motivations seem heartfelt but also seem to have missed the mark. God responds to David through the prophet Nathan by saying that not only does he not dwell in the sort of house that David has in mind, but that his designs are to make a house out of David and his posterity. This can be seen as a prefiguring of First Peter 2:4–5 that speaks of God's unusual building design: "Come to him, a living stone, though rejected by mortals yet chosen and precious in God's sight, and like living stones, let yourselves be built into a spiritual house, to be a holy priesthood." And this rejection of Jesus—the living cornerstone, the chosen one laid by God but rejected by builders (1 Pet 2:6–8)—can be seen as a continuation of the false-self narrative that resists cooperating with the builder of the true house. As we saw in the section above, we are called to be a living, holy dwelling place for the Spirit of God.

Nehemiah, who encounters burnt and dusty rubble in Jerusalem on his return from Babylon (Neh 1:1–11), and Amos (9:11), who describes the fallen booth of David, both suggest that the builders of false houses have indeed labored in vain. This same futility is noted by Jesus, himself a living stone, in his prophecy that "not one stone will be left here upon another" (Matt 24:2). He says this in response to his disciples who thought it necessary to call his attention to the impressive architecture of the temple. The language is eschatological but reinforces the point that we should focus on internal, metaphorical houses that are built upon the rock that is Christ (Matt 7:24–27).

And yet surely this dark, chaotic picture cannot be the last word; surely the one who said that his Father's house has "many dwelling places" (John 14:2) has a more orderly and positive horizon toward which we can aim our hope. Despite opposition, Nehemiah was able to clear the rubble, rebuild the walls, and welcome back the exiles (Neh 6–8). Amos is also hopeful: "On that day I will . . . raise up its ruins, and rebuild it as in the days of old" (Amos 9:11). This and other restoration images are echoed in Robin Mark's popular song, "Days of Elijah": David rebuilds the "temple of praise," and we are called to be laborers in God's vineyard, cultivating fruit as we look to the one who shines "like the sun."[6] Darkness and disarray do not have the final say.

Discerning the Body of Love, the Order of the House

To work with God in his building projects we need to understand our own houses as well as his designs. Recently, I have begun working on a Rule of Life in an effort to order my days in a manner best suited to my calling.[7] One such spiritual practice I observe as a Benedictine oblate is following a weekly schedule of chanting the Psalms. Each time Psalm 27 comes up, I'm drawn to this verse to use as my personal Rule: "One thing I asked of the Lord, that will I seek after: to live in the house of the Lord all the days of my life" (Ps 27:4).

Crafting a Rule of Life in alignment with God's building design for his house is both inspiring and elusive, requiring attention and discernment. David's discovery that God prefers a tent to a splendid temple challenges us to be aware of the movements of this "God of No Fixed Address": "For he will hide me in his shelter in the day of trouble; he will conceal me under the cover of his tent; he will set me high on a rock. . . . I will offer in his tent sacrifices with shouts of joy; I will sing and make melody to the Lord" (Ps 27:5–6). Not only is his temple a tent, a gathering place for pilgrims, it is pitched right in the middle of danger, surrounded by enemies—a place that paradoxically becomes a place of safety where sacrifices of joy and music are offered.

---

6. Mark, "Days of Elijah."

7. Editor's note: see Macchia, *Crafting a Rule of Life*. This practice is associated with Benedictine spirituality, either as a member of a monastic community or as laity (the latter are called oblates, meaning "offering"); e.g., de Waal, *Life-Giving Way*.

There is a further paradox in beginning to understand how the Lord builds the house. Our hearts are often drawn toward pilgrimage, but God uses the stationary stability of our homes as building blocks of the spiritual house where acceptable sacrifices are to be offered. Teresa of Avila challenges us along these same lines: "Can any evil be greater than the evil that we find in our own house? What hope can we have of being able to rest in other people's homes if we cannot rest in our own? . . . Believe me, unless we have peace and strive for peace in our own home, we shall not find it in the homes of others."[8] This stingingly realistic admonition could easily cause us to be discouraged, given the relational disarray we all experience. It's also not hard to see how the weakness of meaningful connections between members of the body of Christ, the body of love, is often what's behind the weakness of its witness.

A strong call to discern this "body of love" persists in my efforts to craft a Rule of Life. Through the Companions of the Sisters of St Joseph, I learned a practice that serves as a template for each "living stone" to share their present State of Heart and Order of the House.[9] This is a sort of corporate examination of conscience, as in Foster's corporate discipline of confession, in which each participant shares what they sense God has been speaking and stirring into their lives. Not only is this practice invaluable for discerning where God may be leading; it also serves to strengthen each person's sense of place within the spiritual house. While stumbling through the rubble of relational breakdown, we are nonetheless able to discern the "body of love" as well as our roles as the new Jerusalem bride (Rev 21:2)—the "true city."

Discerning where this body is being formed, and the Order of the House, requires us to develop an attentiveness to God's presence, and our amazing capacity to be mediators of that presence—"the glory of this mystery, which is Christ in you, the hope of glory" (Col 1:27). Such discerning inevitably involves an increasing awareness that it is the "Lord's doing . . . marvelous in our eyes" (Ps 118:23) as he aligns living stones into the house being built around the rejected cornerstone.

Psychologist David Benner, in *Presence and Encounter*, points out that presence, both human and divine, is often elusive. He offers this inspiring insight into the mysterious ways God's presence manifests: "A person's presence will always be less differentiated and more global than his or

---

8. Teresa of Avila, *Interior Castle*, 68.
9. Cogil et al, "State of the Heart."

her personality. It is as if the presence is less 'owned' than it is Presence mediated."[10] We could see this as another way of understanding our bodies as temples of the Holy Spirit (1 Cor 6:19)—the glory in each of us, the glory in the house, the glory in the city walled with fire.

I see this mediated presence as the active ingredient of prayer walking, and the sort of "Loitering with Intent" that Jill Weber speaks of in her chapter. Time and again we sense that a shift in particular places is connected in some mysterious way to the hope of glory having passed through those places in somebody's temple of the Holy Spirit. To extrapolate from my opening song:

> *Where the Body of Love is being formed, broken hearts are being softened and warmed —*
>
>> In the vision of Open Homes Hamilton, which is making ours a city of mercy and welcome.
>>
>> In a Lenten service of remembrance in the 541 Eatery and Exchange to say prayers, play music, and light candles for friends lost in the opioid crisis.
>>
>> In the various cohorts that have come together in GOHOP's Studies in New Monasticism Internship and Prayer, and Justice and Mission initiatives.
>>
>> In a cell block meeting room in the Barton Street Detention Centre with a raucous rendition of "Nothing but the Blood"[11] bouncing around the concrete walls.
>>
>> In the streets, or city parks, or at a popular waterfront cafe as we reconnect with friends we've not been in contact with through the pandemic.
>
> *—The membrane grows thinner between these streets and the healing unseen.*

The Redemptive Presence of Living Stones

A number of years ago, I joined some friends in a building that had once been a bar with an infamous reputation. New Hope Church held several evenings of prayer and worship in this place and, on this particular

---

10. Benner, *Presence and Encounter*, 5.
11. Lowry, "Nothing but the Blood," public domain.

occasion, an animated rendition of "Let the Flame Burn Brighter" was released into its stale beer and cigarette smoke atmosphere. More recently, I was having a coffee on a bench facing this building, now being transformed by Indwell, a Christian charity that creates affordable housing communities to support people seeking health, wellness, and belonging. A friend who works with Indwell joined me with her sleeping newborn baby—a serendipitous, shared moment watching another "marvelous in our eyes" transformation taking place.

I love the redemptive "living stones meets bricks and mortar" impact that this ministry has had on our city. Like other Indwell projects, such as a former banquet center that had devolved into a haunt of drug and sex trafficking, and like the Playhouse that became a home for CityKidz, this building has witnessed much darkness and human degradation. The transformation of these places has risen, in part, from the capacity of the people who dwell in the light of God's house to carry his presence into the heart of dark, splintered spaces. Interestingly, both "home" and "dwell" are derived from the word "tabernacle," used as both noun and verb.[12] This is another pilgrim paradox: it's in both the noun of staying in the shelter of his tent, and the verb of heading out, waltzing mercy with hearts on fire, that we'll find the body of love being formed. It illustrates the ongoing rhythms of spiritual discipline and mission—the first occurring in the stability of being in God's presence; the second occurring in the movement of mediating that presence. And, of course, they are intertwined as we pray and walk.

As I wander city streets, Miss Gracie in hand, I marvel at the mystery of redemption. A mystery no more comprehensible than dry bones becoming as flesh (Ezek 7:1–14) or Jesus describing his body as a temple being rebuilt in three days after seeming to have been destroyed by death (Mark 8:31; 14:58). The chimes of redemption we are singing and speaking into seeming emptiness ring out in resonance with the loud voice from the throne that heralds the new Jerusalem bride coming down from heaven: "See, the home of God is among mortals. He will dwell with them; they will be his people, and God himself will be with them" (Rev 21:3).

---

12. Editor's note: The classic use of "tabernacle" as a verb is in John 1:14, describing the Word that "lived among us"—the Greek term is literally "tabernacled." E.g., Koester, *Dwelling of God*.

Bibliography

Beale, G. K. *The Temple and the Church's Mission: A Biblical Theology of the Dwelling Place of God*. NSBT 17. Downers Grove, IL: InterVarsity, 2004.

Benner, David. *Presence and Encounter: The Sacramental Possibilities of Everyday Life*. Grand Rapids: Brazos, 2014.

Cogil, Kvale, et al. "State of the Heart and Order of the House: A Way of Nonviolence." Bearers of the Tradition Phase II, 2005. https://cssjfed.org/images/2017_spirituality_section/State_of_the_Heart_-_Order_of_the_House.pdf.

De Waal, Esther. *A Life-Giving Way: A Commentary on the Rule of St. Benedict*. Collegeville, MN: Liturgical, 1995.

Ediger, Gerald C. "The Proto-Genesis of the March for Jesus Movement, 1970–87," *Journal of Pentecostal Theology* 12.2 (2004) 247–75.

Fee, Gordon D. *God's Empowering Presence: The Holy Spirit in the Letters of Paul*. Peabody, MA: Hendrickson, 1994.

Holvast, René. *Spiritual Mapping in the United States and Argentina, 1989–2005: A Geography of Fear*. Leiden: Brill, 2008.

Kendrick, Graham. "Let the Flame Burn Brighter." Track 7 on *Make Way for the Cross*. Make Way Music, 1989.

Koester, Craig R. *The Dwelling of God: The Tabernacle in the Old Testament, Intertestamental Jewish Literature, and the New Testament*. CBQ Monograph 22. Washington: Catholic Biblical Association of America, 1989.

Lowry, Robert. "Nothing but the Blood of Jesus." Public domain, 1876.

Macchia, Stephen A. *Crafting a Rule of Life: An Invitation to the Well-Ordered Way*. Downers Grove, IL: InterVarsity, 2012.

Mark, Robin. "Days of Elijah." Track 1 on *Days of Elijah*. Song Solutions Daybreak, 1996.

Teresa of Avila. *Interior Castle*. Christian Classics. Notre Dame: Ave Maria, 2007.

Tigchelaar, Peter. "Aching for Dawn." 3rd movement of *Healing Suite for Hamilton in E Major*. Urban Green Music, 2009.

Conclusion

— E. JANET WARREN

IT IS FITTING THAT chapter 1 of this book emphasized that the content of the songs we sing is critical—our worship should be directed toward the only true God. And chapter 8 offered some literal examples of redemptive songs that we can sing into the splintered spaces of our world. The chapters in between, sung by many different voices in the choir of contributors, explored various rhythms of mission and spirituality, as expressed through the disciplines, albeit broadly interpreted. Literal singing intertwines with metaphorical. Spiritual practices interweave with missional activities, and are often reciprocal.

Various authors have addressed these questions and more. I have been encouraged and inspired by their knowledge, wisdom, and experience. By their stories detailing the missional fruits that bloom from spiritual disciplines. The songs that help fill splintered spaces. I wonder if this book is not only *about* spiritual disciplines and mission, but that even the writing and reading of it may *be* a spiritual discipline with missional implications and applications.

I have also been convicted by the content of the various chapters. Many of my own attitudes and actions fall short. I may practice spiritual disciplines, but often in a "checking the box" sort of way. Hours and hours of Bible study? Practicing the presence? Practicing hospitality? Being with the least of these?

We hope that readers may be inspired and encouraged through this volume to sing their own songs into their own local and global spaces. And to know that what we sing matters. Who we sing to matters. How we prepare for singing matters. When, where, what, and why we sing matters.

Why We Sing

First, we sing because it flows naturally from following Jesus. Our hearts are filled with harmony. The Bible and Christian history are filled with song. And, paradoxically, this praise draws us closer in our relationship with the Lord and transforms us. Worship, whether through literal song or not, is a spiritual discipline. As Dave Witt notes in his chapter on missional discipleship, we can easily burn out if we fail to balance the rhythms of mission and spirituality. It is especially important that we "sing" and discern the Lord's presence and direction in the context community.

Indeed, many authors discuss the concept of the mysterious but faithful divine presence. In chapter 5, I suggest that practicing mindfulness, being in the present moment, can increase our awareness of God's presence and action. Similarly, Jill Weber and Peter Tigchelaar talk about Christ's redemptive presence and our responsibility in incarnating and mediating it. We need to be intentional about making space for the Holy Spirit to sing through us. This, of course, echoes David Fitch's concept of God's faithful presence that we can simultaneously experience and enact.

Second, and following from this, we sing because we are called to "fill the nation with [the Lord's] song."[1] Worship has outward as well as inward dimensions. Spirituality motivates and sustains mission. By aligning ourselves, through thought and deed, with God's work, we speak to the world. And this world, despite its busyness and noisiness, is needy and empty. It is splintered like rubble from a collapsed building, hearts that have been wounded in many places, lives that are repeatedly dislocated, time that has no rhythm. Our world needs repair and restoration, structure and stability. People long for profound pieces and true tones; we hunger for harmony. Or, in Tigchelaar's words, we are "aching for dawn."

In my introductory chapter, I mention "hurry sickness" and other problems in contemporary society, and in my chapter on mindfulness I discuss the "outer shouts" and "inner doubts" that plague us. Christians are not immune. Indeed, we are often afraid of what we may discover in silence and slowness. Weber, in her chapter on hospitality, refers to our aversions to waiting and being interrupted. Being aware of these

---

1. Kendrick, "Let the Flame Burn Brighter."

issues—in ourselves and others—allows us to engage in mission more effectively. Tigchelaar points out that often we need to tear down "false houses" before we can build true ones.

So we sing. We sing as a way to fill the greatest command (Matt 22:37–40), because we are loved and we love. We sing as a way to fill the great commission (Matt 28:18–20), expressing that love so that others may hear the truth. As we sing, "All the broken and dislocated pieces—people and things, animals and atoms—get properly fixed and fit together in vibrant harmonies" (Col 1:20, MSG).

What We Sing

We sing the way, the truth, and the life (John 14:6). The indwelling presence of the Holy Spirit enables true worship. We sing to the "lion and the lamb," the king who is "clothed in majesty."[2] This may seem obvious, but it is essential that we direct our voices correctly. As Michael Gorman so poignantly notes, in his chapter on cruciformity, the idolatry of nationalism is persuasive and pervasive. Avoiding it is a form of abstinent engagement; it requires us to be countercultural. We need to sing light into the darkness that "tries to hide."[3] It is only through singing and practicing cross-shaped disciplines that we will be filled with the Spirit of God. Through prayer, we encounter the crucified Christ; through mission, we dismiss our own desires and submit ourselves to the ways of the cross.

Somewhat similarly, Michael Knowles points out that the posture and content of our prayers matters. It is not about our own, often selfish mission, but about submitting ourselves to God and his will, joining with the Son and Spirit who are already praying. And so we sing songs of redemption and restoration. Songs of salvation and compassion. We are privileged to be given the ministry of reconciliation, to be called to mediate the voice of love, peace, and truth. The one who wants to reconcile all things to himself (2 Cor 5:18; Col 1:20).

---

2. Tomlin et al., "How Great Is Our God."
3. Tomlin et al., "How Great Is Our God."

How We Sing

All voices benefit from training. Through the various writers in this book, we have learned multiple ways to sing truth, to love God, and to love our neighbors. We have learned how to prepare spiritually for missional activities. We present ourselves to God in order to be transformed. We sit with Jesus then we walk with him into the world, joining him in his mission. Spirituality is within mission and mission is within spirituality. This concept is implicit in all chapters. The ideas of reflexive praxis (Witt's missional discipleship), spiritual attunement (my chapter on mindfulness), and prayer walking (Smith's neighborhood engagement, Weber's loitering with intent, and Tigchelaar's redeeming the city) especially illustrate the interconnectedness of mission and spiritual disciplines. Being aware of the need for the former and being intentional with the latter is how we can "sing the Lord's song in a foreign land" (Ps 137:4).

Some authors address classic spiritual disciplines directly. Not surprisingly, the most common one mentioned is prayer. Knowles reminds us that this involves listening and waiting, not just speaking. God initiates prayer and we respond to him through prayer. Thus, we both spiritually encounter the Lord, and join him in his mission. In my chapter, I suggest some specific types of training, such as breath prayers and the game of minutes. Aaron Smith shares some insights on prayer developed in a missional context. He notes that neighborhood engagement makes our prayers more specific and meaningful. And praying for others helps us to love them better, thus helping us become more Christlike. Jill Weber gives examples of both overt (a poster: "Need Prayer?") and covert (silent supplications for passersby) prayer.

There are also spiritual disciplines that are related to prayer. Knowles and Warren refer to silence; Warren and Weber discuss solitude; Witt, Knowles, and McGuire reference submission; and Gorman and Tigchelaar mention worship, albeit in different contexts. The discipline of guidance or spiritual discernment, perhaps a form of listening prayer, is discussed by Warren, Weber, and Witt. Through mindful attention, being present in the moment, we can better recognize and respond to the voice of God; noting *kairos* moments, seeing where God is working, and joining him in his mission. Discernment is best done within the Christian community.

Scripture study is another discipline that enables us to commune with the Lord. As Seán McGuire points out, it is not just learning *about* the triune God but is a way we can *know* him. When done with depth and commitment, it inspires and illuminates our action in the world. Through study, and articulating what we learn, we become more Christlike and consequently more missional. On a practical level, Smith notes that studying the Bible with others allows us to both grow in our own faith and engage our neighbors. He also mentions the disciplines of fasting (associated with justice) and confession (requiring a change of attitude), both of which indirectly relate to prayer.

Finally, the discipline of service, related to Fitch's idea of "being with the least of these," is mentioned by many authors. Weber and Tigchelaar share their experience of simply being present to people in the vulnerable, splintered spaces in our cities, making space and mediating God's presence. Smith points out that service is not just about sharing meals with neighbors or caring for their children, but may include advocacy and community change. It involves concrete actions more than warm feelings. It is interesting that, although McGuire and Gorman both mention the importance of overtly proclaiming the Gospel (another of Fitch's disciplines), many authors suggest that mission work may be effectively done implicitly as we carry and enact the Lord's redemptive presence. And this, of course, is best accomplished through spiritual disciplines.

There are, of course, many other spiritual disciplines, not explicit in this book, that intertwine with missional activities. Consider sacrifice, simplicity, tithing, creation care, Sabbath keeping, and celebrating the Eucharist. Some of the principles and examples we have shared can easily transfer to other Christian spiritual and missional practices.

Spiritual disciplines help us to be more aware of God, ourselves, and others. They help us become the sort of people God wants for his mission. They help us cultivate Christ-centered identity and community. They are fluid and flexible, but require attention and intention. Remember that disciplines are not work but are practices that disciples of Christ undertake. Fortunately, and paradoxically, the Spirit inspires and enables us to develop healthy spiritual habits. We abide in him and he abides in us. Thus, we bear fruit.

Many spiritual practices have personal benefits, both physical and spiritual, but making us feel good is not their primary intent. Spiritual disciplines will be empty unless they are cruciform. Instead, the rhythms of spirituality and mission are about carrying God's presence, building his kingdom, and joining him in his mission to reconcile humanity to himself. But, in reciprocal fashion, in order to translate and facilitate God's love and truth, we have to know it ourselves first. Missional work needs to be properly grounded within spiritual practices and communities. This is how we sing.

Where and When We Sing

As many authors remind us, God is not confined to buildings or any particular place. Therefore, we sing at all times in all places. We sing alone and we sing with and to others. We sing in buildings and we march in streets. We sing in silent prayer and study. We sing in a prayer truck, with friends at dinner, at a TrueCity conference, and in our local neighborhoods.

As we sing, we tap rhythms—rhythms of worship and work, prayer and practice. We maintain a delicate balance between being still and being active, between listening and speaking, between solitude and community, between receiving and giving, between faith and deeds, between spiritual and missional practice. We come to know God through prayer and study; this in turn enables us to better serve him and understand his mission. As we serve him and others, we too grow spiritually.

Singing is often accompanied by dancing—mostly metaphorical in our context! Recall the movements of mission we discussed in the introduction: spatial and temporal, inward and outward. Through intentional study and prayer, inviting strangers to share a meal, speaking out against idolatry and injustice, or just sitting on a bench with a stranger, we join Jesus as he works to reunite and reconcile the time and space that have become fragmented, as he repairs the splintered spaces of our lives. Looking to him, we sing outward and dance through the districts of our wounded world.

We represent only a small part of the universal choir—one that is much more diverse. We are musical instruments of divine grace, if in need of better tuning at times. As we open our mouths to sing, our hearts and minds are filled with the Spirit. We sing songs that are always new; songs that are appropriate to particular places and times; songs that the deaf can hear; songs that reach far but simultaneously nurture our spirits.

This hymn from the World Council of Churches reflects well the rhythms of mission and spiritual disciplines and resonates with much that we have discussed:[4]

---

4. World Council of Churches, "Companions in the Spirit."

Come Holy Spirit!
settle with your truth
the walls we have built
and open a way
to wander with you
Come Holy Spirit
disturb the familiar
with your odd and other ways
consume our coldness
in the brightness of your flame.
Come Holy Spirit
inspire us to see you
in places that hide you
and summon us to witness
always at your side.
Come Holy Spirit
nourish us with your light
water us with your tears
that your fruit may grow
to create new life.
Go Holy Spirit
lead and leave us again
push us on our way
send us to our neighbors
and Creation's future day.

Bibliography

Kendrick, Graham. "Let the Flame Burn Brighter." Track 7 on *Make Way for the Cross*. Make Way Music, 1989.

Tomlin, Chris, et al. "How Great Is Our God." Track 3 on *Arriving*. Sparrow, 2004.

World Council of Churches. "Companions in the Spirit—Companions in Mission: Reflections on Mission and Spirituality." *International Review of Mission* 101.1 (2012) 43–60.

www.ingramcontent.com/pod-product-compliance
Lightning Source LLC
Chambersburg PA
CBHW021935160426
43195CB00011B/1101